Karen Houghton

FUNDING YOUR MISSION

The Modern Guide to Nonprofit Finance

STONE CREST

STONE CREST
www.stonecrestbooks.com

Stone Crest | www.stonecrestbooks.com

Funding Your Mission
© Copyright 2025 Karen Houghton
By Karen Houghton

First Edition

Published in the United States by Stone Crest Books
www.stonecrestbooks.com
An imprint of Dinosaur House

ISBN:
978-1-961462-37-3 (paperback)
978-1-961462-38-0 (hardcover)
978-1-961462-39-7 (eBook)

Publishing Manager: Stone Crest Books
An imprint of Dinosaur House

Printed in the United States of America

For the nonprofit leaders who show up day after day;
the visionaries, volunteers, board members, and staff
who carry heavy burdens with open hands.

You serve with grit and grace.
You believe in something bigger, and you make it real.

This book is for you.
To equip you, encourage you, and remind you
funding your mission is not a luxury, it's a lifeline.

And to the Infinite Giving team – thank you
for believing in this vision
and helping nonprofits
turn stewardship into strength.

CONTENTS

FOREWORD

It is with great pleasure that I introduce *Funding Your Mission – The Modern Guide to Nonprofit Finance*, a book that fills a critical gap in nonprofit financial management. As a researcher and educator, I have spent much of my career studying the intersection of finance, philanthropy, and nonprofits. I have worked with countless organizations to better understand how they can unlock the full potential of their resources to further their missions.

Over the years, one of the most pressing issues I have encountered is the need for nonprofit leaders to adopt a more strategic approach to financial management. Too often, organizations focus primarily on short-term survival to raise enough money to meet payroll or keep the lights on. While this is important, it often leads to a reactive, crisis-driven mindset, rather than one that proactively seeks to align financial decisions with long-term organizational goals.

The result is nonprofits operating in constant financial desperation. They chase immediate cash donations to fund immediate spending needs. This creates a culture of scarcity and survival, not stability and growth. It leads to exhaustion, burnout, and employee turnover that's notoriously high in the nonprofit sector.

But there is a better way.

In my research, I have found that nonprofits prioritizing long-term financial resilience are more successful in fulfilling their missions. For example, organizations with robust endowment funds tend to have more stable revenue streams, less reliance on cyclical donations, and greater capacity to weather economic downturns. My studies show that nonprofits with diversified investments, both in terms of asset classes and funding sources, are able to endure market fluctuations more effectively.

Nonprofits do not need to continually scramble for disposable income donations to be spent immediately. Instead, they can embrace a sustainable future. This future relies on thoughtful stewardship of both the donors' and the organization's assets and wealth.

A critical finding of my work is the importance of incorporating asset-based giving into nonprofit financial strategies. My research has shown that **nonprofits receiving stock donations experience a 55% increase in fundraising contributions** compared to those relying solely on cash donations. Nonprofits that embrace these gifts not only enhance their fundraising potential but also allow their donors to give in a more tax-efficient manner.

The truth is clear: your nonprofit deserves to thrive, not just survive.

But many nonprofits are unaware of the potential power of wealth sharing and wealth management, not just disposable income sharing and immediate expenditures. By managing these assets strategically, nonprofits can shift from survival to strength.

In *Funding Your Mission*, Karen Houghton offers a practical, actionable roadmap for nonprofit leaders who wish to move beyond traditional fundraising. As the CEO of Infinite Giving, Karen has worked with numerous organizations to build investment strategies that promote financial resilience while staying true to their core mission. This book provides essential insights into cash flow management, portfolio construction, and how to engage donors with non-cash gifts. These strategies are increasingly critical in today's economic environment.

This book is particularly timely, as we are on the brink of the largest wealth transfer in history. An estimated $124 trillion will shift from Baby Boomers to younger generations in the next two decades, and nonprofits that fail to engage with this new donor class will be left behind. I have long emphasized the importance of engaging donors through innovative giving strategies, such as the acceptance of non-cash gifts and the use of donor-advised funds (DAFs). *Funding Your Mission* elaborates on these strategies, providing clear guidance on how nonprofits can not only accept these gifts but also steward them for long-term impact.

Karen's thoughtful approach to financial management is evident throughout the book, particularly in her focus on the importance of reserves and the concept of "balance sheet bravery". By encouraging nonprofits to view strong reserves as a sign of courage rather than conservatism, this helps leaders to move beyond the false dichotomy of "mission vs. money" and adopt a more strategic view of their financial future. As someone who has spent years advocating for the importance of financial sustainability in the nonprofit sector, I wholeheartedly endorse this message.

Another key strength of *Funding Your Mission* is Karen's ability to make financial concepts accessible to nonprofit leaders who may feel intimidated by the complexities of investing and financial reporting. She provides clear, actionable steps for building and managing nonprofit portfolios, aligning investments with mission-driven goals, and creating transparency in financial reporting. Ultimately, Karen is on a mission to empower nonprofit leaders to make informed, confident decisions about their financial futures.

Nonprofits must not only raise funds but also manage and grow them wisely to ensure long-term sustainability. By using tools such as investment policy statements (IPS) and understanding asset allocation, nonprofit leaders can secure their organizations' financial futures while advancing their missions.

I strongly recommend *Funding Your Mission* for nonprofit leaders who seek to build resilient organizations capable of navigating the complexities of modern financial management. The strategies and insights presented here will not only help organizations survive but also thrive in a rapidly changing world. This book is an invaluable resource for nonprofit leaders who are ready to take a proactive, strategic approach to managing their financial resources.

Together, we can move beyond a nonprofit world focused on immediate survival. We can build a sustainable future.

Welcome to Funding Your Mission.

Russell James III, JD, Ph.D., CFP®
Professor, Charitable Financial Planning,
School of Financial Planning, Texas Tech University

*Dr. Russell James is not a current client of Infinite Giving nor was he provided compensation for his contribution. We are extremely grateful for his work in our industry.

CHAPTER 1

Rethinking Nonprofit Finance

Let's transform how nonprofits manage and grow their finances.

When I founded my nonprofit, I believed deeply in its mission. I poured my heart and soul into fundraising, programming, and serving our community. Like so many nonprofit leaders, I believed hard work, passion, and purpose could carry us through anything.

But I quickly discovered something discouraging: that mindset was not enough. Like many nonprofits, we were doing big, important work, but we were also operating month-to-month, clinging to every dollar, and trying to do more with less. We praised our "lean" budget and "low overhead," but behind the scenes, this scarcity mindset was burning people out, myself included.

That experience became a turning point. I realized that caring for communities also meant building financial systems that could sustain them. Scarcity, no matter how well-intentioned, was not a strategy. The people we served wanted to ensure we would be there in the long term.

That's where the vision for Infinite Giving was born: out of frustration with instability and a desire to help nonprofits build the continuity and financial strength that is so accepted and commonplace in other sectors.

When unexpected challenges hit, the cracks in our systems widen. Nonprofits watch funding dry up if events are canceled, grants are delayed, or other circumstances outside their control shift suddenly. Organizations doing critical, life-saving work can find themselves at risk through no fault of their own.

It's heartbreaking. However, it also reveals something urgent: nonprofits need better tools and more effective strategies.

Not just more donations. Not just bigger events. They need similar financial frameworks and systems that the for-profit world has long relied on: diversified revenue, accessible investment opportunities, flexible reserves, and better technology.

What Businesses Get Right

In the for-profit world, companies are expected to plan for growth. They take risks, raise capital, and build systems that scale. Startups routinely leverage angel investors, recurring revenue, and financial forecasting tools. They don't apologize for building reserves – they celebrate it.

So why shouldn't nonprofits do the same? Yes, donor dollars need careful stewardship. Yes, tax-exempt status comes with complexity. And yes, the expectations placed on nonprofit leaders are much higher (and less forgiving) than those in the business world.

But the need for financial strength, stability, and vision is just as vital. If anything, it's even more important.

If your mission matters, your financial strength should match it.

Nonprofits deserve the same level of financial confidence and infrastructure as any other sector. They should be able to forecast cash flow, absorb economic shocks, and pursue a long-term vision.

And yet, 90% of U.S. nonprofits don't even have a brokerage account. That means they can't accept gifts of stock or invest the cash they've worked so hard to raise. Not because nonprofit leaders lack skill or vision, but because there are too many systemic barriers to make them widely accessible.

Opening a brokerage account as a nonprofit can take months, compared to the minutes it takes a business or individual. Many institutions set prohibitively high minimums or turn nonprofits away altogether because they don't see them as profitable clients. Add to that the fear many boards and leaders feel about "being in the market," worrying that investing reserves as a nonprofit is too risky. Losing money is seen as poor stewardship; thus, you have a recipe for paralysis.

But there is also real risk in doing nothing, letting inflation quietly erode the value of donor dollars. To move forward, nonprofits must overcome both systemic barriers and cultural fear, reclaiming investment not as speculation but as wise stewardship that strengthens their mission.

Traditional Financial Systems and Nonprofits

The U.S. financial system was built for individuals and for-profit businesses, not tax-exempt organizations. **Tax-exempt organizations face systemic roadblocks at every turn.**

You might wait months just to open a brokerage account. You might have to personally guarantee your organization's credit card. You might spend weeks just trying to change a name on an account. This pain point occurs more often than many realize due to staff turnover and transitioning board members at the end of their respective terms. These may seem like small things, but for nonprofit leaders, they add up to one message: *the U.S. financial system wasn't built for us.*

And unless you're deeply steeped in nonprofit finance, you may never even realize how different the rules are. This is where the frustration lies for so many smart, capable nonprofit leaders and where the opportunity begins.

These aren't just minor inconveniences. They are systemic barriers that slow down generosity, stall financial growth, and leave even well-run organizations stuck in reactive mode.

Ultimately, these infrastructure limitations leave a lot of smart, well-meaning, often overworked people trying to navigate a system that simply wasn't built for them. We're trying to fit tax-exempt entities into financial processes that assume for-profit norms, and it doesn't work.

And this is an industry where financial stewardship is perhaps the most important.

That's the gap I set out to close.

From Startups to Stewardship

My career path took me from nonprofit leadership into corporate social responsibility and eventually into the tech and venture capital world. I've seen billions of dollars flow through the tech ecosystem, funding moonshot ideas. And all the while, I carried one question with me...

Why don't nonprofits (who are solving society's most urgent problems) have access to the same tools and opportunities these for-profit companies do?

I knew how to build technology. I understood how capital markets work. But more than anything, I understood nonprofits: their urgency, their constraints, and their deep sense of responsibility.

So, we created Infinite Giving not just as a technology platform, but as a fiduciary partner: mission-aligned, intuitive, and built from the ground up specifically for nonprofit leaders.

Along the way, I was introduced to the idea of *redemptive entrepreneurship* by building businesses that restore what's been lost or broken. "Redemption," at its root, is an economic term. It means to buy something back and restore it to its rightful place.

What if we could do that for nonprofit finance? What if we could reclaim generosity as something powerful, abundant, *and* practical? What if we could build organizations that were not just surviving but sustainable and thriving, and we were given permission to celebrate that?

That's why Infinite Giving exists. And that's why I wrote this book.

Because I believe the most world-changing missions deserve the strongest financial foundations. And I believe in our ability to build them, one wise, intentional step at a time.

A New Nonprofit Financial Framework

This book is a roadmap, written with big heart and deep hope, for leaders like you who are doing the hard, important work. You won't find fluff or jargon here, just real tools, honest encouragement, and a shared belief that your mission deserves every bit of strength and strategy it can get.

You'll find mindset shifts that move you from scarcity to strategy. You'll find frameworks for building reserves, investment policies, and risk-aligned portfolios. You'll find practical tools, from board-level talking points to donor communication scripts, to help you implement and advocate for change.

But more than anything, I hope this book gives you permission.

Permission to think bigger. To speak more boldly about money. To lead with both heart and more financial clarity.

Because when you're equipped with the right tools and language, you can:

- Confidently lead your board and staff into financial conversations

- Attract and retain generous donors who want to give in impactful ways

- Build a nonprofit that's not just reacting but planning, growing, and sustaining for the long haul

A Vision for the Future

My hope is that one day soon:

- Every nonprofit has a reserve strategy they're proud of

- Investment conversations are common in boardrooms, not feared

- Stock gifts, crypto, and donor-advised funds are embraced with ease

- And most importantly, nonprofits no longer feel guilty about having money, but feel empowered to steward it well

Because money isn't the enemy of mission. It's the fuel that makes the work possible.

Whether you're an executive director juggling a dozen hats, a seasoned CFO managing a thin margin, a brand-new Treasurer learning the ropes, or a board member with decades of banking or financial experience, this book is for you.

Nonprofit finance is its own discipline. From brokerage requirements and investment policy statements to donor-advised funds, reserve strategy, and endowment structure—the rules, risks, and responsibilities are different. Even financial professionals on boards are often navigating unfamiliar territory without the tailored guidance they need.

This book brings that guidance. It offers tools, language, and frameworks designed specifically for the nonprofit world. So, whether you're new to financial leadership or steeped in it, there's something here for you.

You are the bridge to a better financial future in the nonprofit sector.

You are built to last. You are built for more.

Let's begin.

Key Takeaways for Your Mission

- **Financial Strength is Mission Strength**
  Just like businesses, nonprofits deserve access to reserves, investments, and forecasting tools that allow them to absorb shocks and pursue vision with confidence.

- **Readiness Unlocks Generosity**
  Without the right accounts and policies, nonprofits miss out on stock gifts, donor-advised funds (DAFs), and other transformational giving vehicles. Building infrastructure signals trust and maturity to donors.

- **A New Framework is Possible**
  By shifting mindset, adopting tailored tools, and giving ourselves permission to steward money boldly, nonprofits can move from survival mode to sustainability and growth.

CHAPTER 2

Money is Not a Dirty Word

Let's just say it out loud: nonprofits need money.

Not hope. Not good intentions. Not just volunteers or visibility. Money.

While nonprofits operate under a different tax status and with a deeper sense of purpose, the financial reality is the same: they are still organizations with payroll to meet, overhead to cover, and people depending on them. They aren't less than businesses; in many ways, they carry even greater responsibility and deliver life-changing work while often being held to higher scrutiny and thinner margins.

Nonprofits exist to serve people, to meet urgent needs, and to bring vision into reality. And yet, for all our passion for impact, one word still makes many leaders shift uncomfortably in their seats: money.

We talk about programming. We talk about outcomes. We talk about community change. But when the conversation turns to finances (reserves, investments, or long-term strategy), the room gets quieter. For many organizations, money feels out of step with the mission. It shouldn't.

Money is not a distraction from your mission. It is the fuel that allows your mission to run.

Without money, vision stays an idea. With it, vision becomes impact.

If your nonprofit is solving real problems, meeting urgent needs, or working to change the world, then you need resources to do that well and sustainably. That means you need to talk about money. You need to build a healthy financial strategy. And you need to free your organization from the false dichotomy that says impact and income must live on opposite sides of the table.

This discomfort didn't come from anywhere. Many of us were raised with complicated narratives around money, stories that praised sacrifice, equated wealth with corruption, or taught us that "doing good" should somehow be separate from "making money." These mindsets, while often well-intentioned, have seeped into nonprofit culture, making it harder to talk about financial health without feeling self-conscious or even guilty.

But here's the hard reality: underfunded missions stay small, and most nonprofits are indeed small. According to the National Council of Nonprofits, 92% of charitable organizations in the U.S. operate with less than $1 million a year. This is why we all have to be more intentional about stewardship. Undercapitalized organizations fold.

That's not virtuous. That's avoidable.

We must begin rewriting the money story in the nonprofit sector. Financial transparency, literacy, and ambition are not luxuries for nonprofits. They are essentials. The ability to manage resources well, to invest in long-term capacity, and to speak openly about funding needs should be seen.

Why Talking About Money Feels So Hard

I'll never forget sitting across the table from a smart, committed Executive Director of a growing nonprofit. Her team was doing transformational work, offering educational support to hundreds of children in underserved neighborhoods, and demand for their programs was only increasing.

But when I asked about their financial reserves, she hesitated.

"We have some," she said, "but I worry about how it looks. If we show too much on our balance sheet, donors might think we don't need their support. And I don't want people to think we're spending too much on overhead."

That quiet fear, the fear of being misunderstood, is all too common. It's actually known as the "overhead myth." Many nonprofit leaders carry an invisible weight: the pressure to appear lean, the fear that transparency around reserves or staff costs might trigger skepticism. Somewhere along the way, the sector adopted an unspoken belief: the less you spend on yourself, the more "pure" your mission.

The fact of the matter is that reserves are not overhead. If you set a policy, it's not an ongoing expense. In fact, reserves can and should be leveraged to provide growth just by existing. They are also there to supplement the mission if/when things don't go as planned.

Here's the thing: no business would be expected to operate without overhead, cash reserves, or competitive salaries. Why should nonprofits be any different?

Together with the Executive Director, we reviewed the nonprofit's financials and reframed her narrative. We helped her board see that healthy reserves weren't a liability, but they were a sign of responsible stewardship. That investing in her team and infrastructure was essential, not optional. That donors don't just give to need; they give to vision, stability, and trust.

With a stronger financial strategy and greater transparency, she was able to grow her annual fundraising by 40% the following year. And her largest donor said something that stuck with her: "I'm not just investing in the children you serve. I'm investing in the long-term strength of your organization."

That's the shift we all need to make. Strong nonprofits shouldn't hide their strength — they should build on it.

3 Reasons Why We're Afraid to Talk About Money

There are a few common reasons nonprofit leaders and more members may shy away from financial conversations, even when they know they're necessary. Here are some that might feel familiar:

1. We're Afraid of Appearing Self-Serving

Nonprofits are driven by mission, not margins. That's the heartbeat of the work. But somewhere along the way, a false story took hold: if you talk too much about money, you're not mission-driven *enough*. If you build reserves, you're "forsaking those you serve." If you invest, you're "trying to get rich."

This mindset creates a false dichotomy between mission and money. And many nonprofits end up operating under a scarcity mindset, living month-to-month and relying on short-term gifts.

For faith-based organizations, the tension can run even deeper. Financial planning may be misunderstood as a lack of trust, rather than what it can truly be: a faithful, biblical approach to stewardship (think of the Parable of the Talents, where resources were multiplied for greater impact). Some even fear that building an endowment or maintaining significant reserves signals "stockpiling" instead of serving.

But I believe this thinking is flawed and shortsighted. Healthy finances are not a distraction from the mission; they are a foundation for it.

Because here's the truth: **strong finances support stronger mission outcomes**. Talking about money doesn't dilute your purpose but empowers it.

2. We Don't Want to Scare Off Donors

There's often an internal fear: *If we admit we're financially strong, donors will stop giving.* But research and real-world results tell a different story.

Dr. Russell James' research found that **perceived financial health significantly increases donor trust and generosity, particularly among high-capacity givers.**[1]

Nonprofits that demonstrate financial strength also tend to keep their donors. The *Fundraising Effectiveness Project* reports that donor retention is consistently higher among

---

[1] *Note - Dr. James has so much wonderful research for nonprofit leaders that is all available to access for free on his website, EncourageGenerosity.com.*

organizations that show stability, transparency, and a long-term plan.

That tells us that donors are more likely to consistently give to organizations that demonstrate financial health, transparency, and a long-term strategy.

We call this balance sheet bravery.

3. We've Been Taught That Money = Overhead

The **Overhead Myth** is the widespread (and harmful) belief that a nonprofit's effectiveness can be judged primarily by how little it spends on "overhead" such as staff salaries, fundraising costs, administrative expenses, or technology rather than on the outcomes it achieves.

Here's why it's a problem:

- **It discourages investment in infrastructure.** Nonprofits may underpay staff, skip technology upgrades, or avoid professional development to keep their "overhead" percentage low, even though these investments could improve programs and expand impact.

- **It misleads donors.** Many assume that a low overhead ratio means donations are "well spent," when in reality, cutting essential administrative costs can actually hurt an organization's ability to deliver results.

- **It punishes growth and innovation.** Expanding programs often requires more staff, better systems, and stronger fundraising, all of which raise overhead but also increase impact.

The term became more widely known after the 2013 *"Letter to the Donors of America"* from GuideStar, Charity Navigator, and the BBB Wise Giving Alliance, which urged donors to stop using overhead ratios as the primary measure of a nonprofit's performance.

In short, the Overhead Myth says, "low overhead = good," but in reality, healthy overhead is often a sign of a strong, sustainable organization.

The aftermath of this myth seems to linger even today. Many organizations still feel pressure to appear as lean and, sometimes, as financially fragile as possible. As a result, strategic investments in areas such as staff, reserves, and infrastructure get lumped in together, especially when things are lean.

It's time to break that cycle. Money isn't the enemy. Mismanagement is.

But wise stewardship? That's part of your job.

Major donors want to give their money to make a lasting impact. It's your role to offer the perfect opportunity to inspire large gifts and planned giving. The ability to tell donors, "Your gift today will support this mission for generations," is a powerful and compelling message.

Reframing the Narrative: What Money *Actually* Is

Let's get one thing straight: **money is not a dirty word. It's directional.**

It reflects values, priorities, and strategy about where you're headed and what you're building. In a nonprofit context, money doesn't compromise mission; instead, it fuels it, pointing your organization toward greater impact, sustainability, and reach. When managed wisely and with intention, money becomes one of your most powerful tools for advancing good.

Today, can you articulate how every dollar received tells this story?

- What do you value?

- What do you prioritize?

- Where are you headed?

If not, this is a great moment to have that conversation with your board and leadership team. You probably have an inherent understanding of your return on investment (ROI) for the funding you receive, but how are you articulating that to your donors? Quantify donations into impact and programs into improved lives.

Having more money doesn't make your organization less pure. And having too little doesn't make your mission more holy.

What matters is how you **align your resources with your responsibilities**. That's not greed. That's leadership.

Let's replace Old Beliefs with New Truths:

Old Belief	New Truth
"Talking about money feels awkward."	"Talking about money builds trust."
"Having reserves looks selfish."	"Having reserves is how we protect our mission."
"Our savings account is fine. Investing is risky."	"Not investing is risky when inflation erodes your dollars."
"We shouldn't profit from donations."	"We should grow gifts so we can do more good."

So how do you get started incorporating these New Truths into the conversations you're having about money? We'll show you how to become fluent in the language of nonprofit finance.

Financial Fluency Is a Leadership Skill

Imagine if a school principal refused to review student performance data because they "weren't a numbers person." Or if a doctor avoided talking about treatment costs because they wanted to "stay focused on the medicine." In both cases, they'd be missing critical information that affects their ability to lead well.

The same is true for nonprofit leaders. Because most nonprofits operate on donations and grants, your ability to understand and communicate financial realities is not optional; it's core to your leadership.

Financial fluency doesn't mean you need a finance degree. It means having the courage, clarity, and confidence to connect your mission to its resources, to make informed decisions, and to lead your organization with both heart and wisdom.

Take Maria, the executive director of a small literacy nonprofit. When a major grant was unexpectedly cut, her team panicked. But because Maria understood their cash flow, reserves, and donor pipeline, she quickly adjusted the budget, communicated transparently with her board, and launched a targeted fundraising appeal. Within two months, the shortfall was covered, and programs continued without interruption.

Every nonprofit will face moments like this: a funding shortfall, an unexpected expense, or a shift in donor priorities. Leaders who understand their numbers can respond quickly, rally support, and protect the mission they serve.

Financial fluency is safeguarding the work you were called to do.

3 Practical Steps to Start Leading Financially

No matter your experience, you can start building confidence and shifting your organization's culture toward financial clarity and strength today. Here's how:

1. Normalize Financial Conversations

Money shouldn't only come up during the annual budget meeting or in response to a crisis. It should be part of your regular dialogue, just like program updates or event planning.

Bring finances (not just fundraising) into staff meetings, leadership discussions, and board agendas early and often. When money becomes a routine part of the conversation, you remove the stigma and create a culture of ownership.

Lead with your mission, but follow with the math. The two belong together. For example:

- "Because of our investment strategy, we were able to maintain programming without interruption."

- "Your gift won't just be used well — it will be grown well."

When your team, board, and donors see the clear link between financial health and mission impact, they're more likely to engage, give, and advocate.

2. Build Shared Language

Not everyone needs to be a finance expert, but everyone should be aligned in mission, goals, and strategy. That starts with a common vocabulary.

Use plain language and define key terms in simple ways:

- "Liquidity" can be explained as "how quickly we can access cash if needed."

- "Operating runway" can be translated to "how many months we can keep serving without new donations coming in."

The more accessible your language, the more likely people are to participate and to spot opportunities or risks earlier. A shared language also makes it easier to onboard new staff, engage board members, and build donor trust. When everyone can talk about money without fear or confusion, you create a team that moves in the same direction with clarity and confidence.

3. Tell the Story Behind the Numbers

Numbers matter, but they're not the story – they're the evidence. Your job as a leader is to connect the two.

Stories engage more parts of the brain than facts alone, especially the amygdala, which processes emotion and memory. That's why a narrative can transform a spreadsheet into something people feel and remember.

Instead of simply reporting, "We have $300,000 in reserves," say: *"We have five months of operating runway, so we can serve our community without interruption, even when funding is delayed."*

That small shift translates a static figure into a sense of stability, foresight, and mission protection. Stories make the impact of your numbers tangible, and they give people a reason to care and a vision for what's possible. And when you consistently tell those stories, you turn your financial updates into tools that can rally support, inspire generosity, and reinforce your organization's credibility.

In summary, donors and board members don't just want data; they want meaning. They want to know why your reserves matter, how your strategy supports growth and sustainability, and what your financial health makes possible.

When you combine transparency with mission-centered storytelling, you create confidence and inspire action. You're not just showing that your organization is surviving, you're showing that you're ready for more.

Key Takeaways for Your Mission

- **Money Doesn't Compete with Your Mission, It Fuels It**
  Nonprofits often fear that talking about money undermines their mission, but the opposite is true. Financial strength empowers long-term impact. Having properly managed reserves and long-term investments isn't greedy, it's good stewardship.

- **Donors Want to Give to Strong, Strategic Organizations**
  Don't hide financial health out of fear that donors will stop giving. The truth is, most donors give more confidently to nonprofits that show transparency, strategy, and stability. Financial strength isn't off-putting; it's reassuring, especially for major gifts.

- **Old Beliefs Around Money Are Holding Us Back**
  It's time to replace our scarcity mindset and overhead myths with truths. Talking about money can build trust, reserves protect your mission, and not investing wisely can sometimes be the riskiest move of all. Follow the data. These strategies work.

- **Financial Fluency Is a Leadership Skill**
  You don't need a finance degree, but you do need to understand and communicate where your money is going, why it matters, and how it supports your mission. Leaders who embrace financial clarity will build stronger, more resilient organizations.

- **Storytelling Leads to Stronger Giving**
  Spreadsheets don't move people, but stories do. Translate technical financial data into meaningful narratives. For example: "We have $500,000 in reserves" becomes "We have six months of runway to serve our community, even during delays." That's what inspires action and trust. Dr. James has a wonderful resource guide about "The Storytelling Fundraiser" that's available on his website EncourageGenerosity.com.

CHAPTER 3

The Journey of Leveling Up: Scarcity → Strategy → Sustainability

Imagine a small nonprofit in a community recovering from a devastating flood. In the early days, the team worked around the clock distributing food, offering shelter, and providing counseling. The local response was generous, and the organization's passion carried them through the worst of it.

But as the weeks passed, donations slowed. Media coverage faded. The crisis receded from public view, but the need on the ground remained. Their bank account, once flush with emergency support, was now dangerously low.

The staff sat around the table, facing impossible decisions. Should they lay off a team member? Cut a critical program? Delay paying a vendor just to get through the next payroll?

There were no easy answers. They hadn't done anything wrong; they'd served their community with compassion and urgency. But they hadn't planned for what came next.

This is the silent failure facing too many nonprofits.

It's rarely a lack of commitment. The real problem is the narrative they've inherited, one that tells them sustainability is selfish, saving is suspect, and strength somehow threatens the purity of their mission.

But here's the truth: that story is costing us impact. And it's time we write a new one, one where strategy fuels generosity, and sustainability becomes the norm, not the exception.

Scarcity is Survival Mode

Scarcity is survival mode. It's reactive. And while every nonprofit begins here, with a vision, a prayer, and a hope, the key is that we can't stay here.

Scarcity shows up in familiar ways:

- "We can't afford to…" becomes the default language.

- Leaders hesitate to invest in infrastructure or staff.

- A burnout culture emerges, expecting more with less.

- Strategic risks are avoided because failure feels too costly.

Too many nonprofits end up stuck in this "hand-to-mouth" cycle—spending every dollar as soon as it comes in, believing it proves their commitment to the cause. In reality, it only highlights the fragility of the system we've built.

There's an urgency in this sector that makes you feel like you have to spend it all now. That if you don't, donors might think you don't need it—or worse, they might stop giving. But constantly reacting instead of planning creates a financial treadmill that wears down even the most passionate teams.

This isn't just a stress point; it's a strategic liability. Without reserves, you can't weather crises, take smart risks, or grow your impact. You're left choosing between today's emergencies and tomorrow's opportunities. Over time, that pressure burns out staff, fractures leadership, and limits your mission.

Why We Must Rethink the Role of Money

In most nonprofits, money is not an off-limits topic, as it comes up often in conversations about fundraising campaigns, project budgets, and urgent needs. But sustainability? That's where the dialogue thins out. We rally donors around a specific initiative or crisis, but rarely around the idea of building long-term financial strength. It's as if talking about reserves or surplus somehow signals we're less committed to the mission, when in reality, it's the very thing that ensures the mission endures.

Let's be clear: money is not the enemy of mission. It is the fuel that allows your mission to run. You cannot serve, grow, or scale without it. The very work that drives your passion for feeding families, advocating for justice, educating children, protecting the planet, you name it, they all require stable funding to thrive.

When we treat money like a necessary evil, we unintentionally train our boards, staff, and donors to see it the same way. But money, when stewarded wisely, is not just acceptable, it's honorable. It enables stability. It sustains impact. It empowers vision.

Think of reserves not as hoarding, but as safeguarding. Not as excess, but as endurance. A nonprofit with reserves can serve longer, plan better, and move faster when opportunities or challenges arise. It can retain staff during lean years, invest in innovation, and step into new initiatives with confidence instead of hesitation.

Financial strength doesn't diminish your mission; it protects it. It ensures that your organization isn't constantly one crisis away from cutting programs or letting people go. And just as importantly, it allows your team to work from a place of hope and creativity, not fear and exhaustion.

And let's just say what often goes unsaid: **scarcity can be a control mechanism**. It keeps organizations dependent, reactive, and hesitant to dream. Breaking that cycle requires courage and a new vision for what responsible, empowered financial leadership looks like.

So, the real question isn't *"Should we build reserves?"*

The real question is: *"Can we afford not to?"*

Because in today's world, uncertainty is certain. What sets resilient nonprofits apart is not luck but leadership with a financial strategy built to last. And that starts with rethinking the role of money, diversifying revenue streams, and opening new pathways of giving.

If you're thinking, *"Great, but how do we do this, Karen?"* Don't worry. I'll provide specific guidelines in Chapter 4.

From Burnout to Breathing Room

One of the most overlooked benefits of a strong financial strategy is the way it protects your people. Teams can't innovate or plan if they're in survival mode. Board members can't focus on governance when they're worried about cash flow. Staff can't stay energized if every week feels like a sprint to cover next week's bills, and donors feel that desperation.

Financial reserves change the tone of the conversation. They give your people breathing room. They create margin for vision. They make leadership sustainable.

You didn't enter this work to play defense every day. You entered it to build something that lasts. And that means you need more than passion; you need planning.

Donors Want Strength, Not Struggle

According to the *U.S. Trust Study of High Net Worth Philanthropy*, 69% of major donors say they're more likely to give to nonprofits that demonstrate strong leadership and clear financial strategy.

In other words, **building reserves builds donor confidence**.

The idea that donors only give when you're in crisis is a myth. Yes, urgent appeals can spark one-time gifts. But your strongest supporters, the ones who give consistently, fund capacity-building, and make transformational gifts, aren't looking to rescue you.

Generous donors don't want to fund a financial hole. **They want to invest in a vision.** A strong one. A strategic one. A sustainable one.

Strategy Is Intentional

Scarcity thinking keeps your mission small. It leads to under-resourcing, staff burnout, and missed opportunities. It convinces you to shrink rather than scale, to apologize rather than advocate, to survive instead of thrive.

It keeps your team in constant reaction mode, scrambling to make payroll, cutting corners, and putting off long-term planning. It teaches your board to fear ambition. And it signals to donors that your organization is fragile.

But strategic thinking? That's where momentum begins.

- It creates a path to resilience

- It empowers you to lead with clarity and confidence

- It builds a culture of generosity that isn't driven by desperation, but by vision

Strategy invites you to zoom out, to build not just for today but for the next chapter. It shifts your posture from scarcity to stewardship. From fragility to resilience.

Strategy creates a path to sustainability. **It's not about having excess, but having enough.** Enough to serve with excellence. Enough to grow without fear. Enough to say yes to the opportunities that align with your mission.

It empowers you to lead with clarity and confidence. To build a culture of generosity that isn't driven by desperation, but by vision.

This is how you build the future, on purpose and with purpose. Not by wishing for more, but by planning for it. Not by asking *"Can we afford this?"* but *"What would it take to make this possible?"*

Even if you desire to stay small, you can still lead big. Everyone has their own path, but nonprofits of all sizes can still build towards legacy.

Beyond Donations: Diversifying Your Revenue

One of the most overlooked strategies for building sustainability is diversifying beyond charitable donations. While generosity will always be your lifeblood, relying on one primary source of income leaves your organization vulnerable to economic shifts, donor attrition, or unexpected crises.

A healthy nonprofit often has multiple revenue streams, which can include:

- **Earned income** from services, ticket sales, or training programs.

- **Membership models** that provide recurring revenue.

- **Strategic partnerships** with corporations or local businesses.

- **Investment income** from reserves, endowments, or other managed funds.

- **Government contracts or grants** that provide stability alongside private giving.

Even small steps in this direction can compound over time. A community theater might offer paid acting classes between productions. An animal shelter could launch a branded merchandise line. A faith-based nonprofit might invest part of its reserves in a conservative portfolio to generate annual income.

Take the example of a small community art center. For years, they relied almost entirely on donations and a couple of annual fundraisers. Then, during a slow giving season, they began offering paid weekend workshops led by local artists. The classes quickly sold out, providing not only an extra $15,000 a year in income but also introducing new people to the organization, many of whom became donors.

That modest stream of earned revenue didn't replace charitable giving, but it smoothed their cash flow, funded needed repairs, and reduced the pressure on their year-end campaign.

The value is not just in the extra dollars; it's in the stability and flexibility those dollars create. Diversified revenue helps you weather downturns, fund innovation, and reduce the pressure on fundraising cycles. It's not about replacing donations; instead, you're strengthening the foundation they're built upon.

Sustainability Is Readiness

Sustainability doesn't mean stockpiling funds or chasing endless growth. It means having what you need to fulfill your mission with strength, flexibility, and courage.

It means:

☐ Having a runway for your programs – not a cliff

☐ Saying yes to opportunity – not just no to crisis

☐ Being ready for the future – not afraid of it

This is not only possible. It's necessary. Sometimes carving out time and resources to achieve this means making short-term cuts for long-term gains. Sustainability means not committing to program growth before building a strong foundation to ensure continuity for the people you serve.

Take, for example, a youth development nonprofit that chose to pause expansion into two new schools. The decision disappointed some stakeholders at the time, but by redirecting funds to build a six-month reserve, they positioned themselves to survive a sudden funding gap the following year.

Because they had prepared, the organization not only kept serving their students but also earned the confidence of a major foundation, which later funded the very expansion they once delayed. That temporary sacrifice became the bridge to long-term growth and stability.

Final Word: Permission to Plan

You don't need anyone's permission to build reserves. But if you've been waiting for it, consider this your green light.

✓ You have permission to think long-term

✓ To prioritize sustainability

✓ To stop apologizing for wanting security

✓ To start building systems that protect your mission, not distract from it

✓ To try something new and diversify your revenue streams

Because no mission thrives on fumes. But when it's backed by strategy and grounded in strength?

That's when sustainability emerges. Let's build toward that future, together.

Key Takeaways for Your Mission

- **Sustainability Is Not Selfish; It's Stewardship**
  Nonprofits have been conditioned to see saving as suspect, but financial strength is a form of responsible leadership. It protects your people, preserves your mission, and fuels long-term impact.

- **Scarcity Thinking Shrinks Missions; Strategy Expands Them**
  Leading from a mindset of lack results in burnout, turnover, and missed opportunities. A strategic approach shifts the focus from survival to sustainability and impact.

- **Donors Trust and Fund Strength, Not Struggle**
  Research shows donors give more (and give more consistently) to organizations that show strong financial leadership and stability. Vision and sustainability inspire generosity more than desperation does.

- **Diversification Builds Resilience**
  A healthy nonprofit explores multiple revenue streams beyond traditional donations, such as earned income, strategic partnerships, investment income, or grants to create stability, reduce vulnerability, and expand opportunity.

- **You Don't Need Permission to Plan for the Future**
  Nonprofit leaders have the right and responsibility to create financial systems that protect their teams, their impact, and their long-term vision.

CHAPTER 4

Understanding Nonprofit Cash Reserves

For many nonprofit leaders, the phrase "cash reserves" can stir discomfort. It might sound like excess to have money sitting idle while urgent programs need funding, or worse, a sign that you're holding back support from the community.

Some boards worry that reserves make them look too financially secure. Others fear that donors expect every dollar to be deployed immediately.

But here's the truth: reserves are not a luxury. They're a responsibility. And having cash reserves is one of the most powerful ways you can protect your mission over the long term.

Still, before you start building a reserve strategy, you need to understand what you're building on. You can't make strong financial decisions without knowing the basic flow of money in and out of your organization.

Too many nonprofits jump straight to questions like "how much should we save?" before they've asked, "what does our cash flow even look like?" Without clarity here, even the best reserve plan won't hold up. You must first know your rhythm: how donations come in, how expenses go out, and where your pressure points lie.

Let's take a few moments to lay the right foundation.

Before You Build: The Basics of Cash Flow

Every strong reserve strategy begins with clarity. That means understanding how your cash actually moves: how and when donations arrive, what bills come due, and which expenses are fixed, flexible, or seasonal.

Nonprofit cash flow isn't linear. A capital campaign might bring in a flood of donations in one quarter and silence the next. Grant payments can be delayed by months, even though payroll and rent don't wait. Meanwhile, your most mission-critical programs often come with unpredictable costs. This uneven rhythm is not a failure in planning; it's a feature of nonprofit life. But ignoring it leads to dangerous assumptions about what's available versus what's sustainable.

Before you start setting aside reserves, take time to map your financial rhythm:

- When do your major donations typically arrive? Monthly? Quarterly? End of year?

- Do your biggest expenses all land at once or spread out evenly?

- Are there "pinch points" when cash is tight, such as just before a grant disbursement?

- How much of your income is reliable versus variable?

This exercise helps you spot the real gaps, those windows of time when you might appear cash-rich on paper, but in reality, you're inching toward red.

It also reveals opportunities to make smarter decisions: delaying a hire until after grant funding clears, setting aside a portion of major gifts for future use, or planning programs around your actual financial runway, not just the annual budget.

By learning the rhythm of your donations, goods, and expenses, you begin to distinguish between true operating costs and excess cash. And once you've identified excess cash, you can put it to work, intentionally and strategically, in a reserve fund designed to support your mission through the ups and downs.

Only once you understand your cash flow can you build a reserve plan that isn't just aspirational but functional.

And that brings us back to why reserves matter so much. Reserves aren't just for the ultra-wealthy. Reserves are an inherent part of a cash management strategy. Not only do they provide a financial cushion for emergencies, but they can also produce additional income. Thoughtful stewardship of what we have been given can create wealth all on its own.

A Story to Break the Stigma

Once you understand your cash flow, the next step is often the hardest one: giving yourself permission to save.

The first time I brought up the idea of building reserves to one of our nonprofit clients, the Executive Director looked at me with wide eyes and shook her head. "We're not a wealthy organization," she said. "We don't just have money sitting around. Our programs need that funding today, not tomorrow."

I understood her hesitation. When your organization is fighting to meet urgent needs every day, setting money aside can feel counterintuitive, maybe even irresponsible. But here's what we discovered together: not building reserves is one of the most dangerous financial moves a nonprofit can make.

She wasn't alone in her concern. Many nonprofit leaders carry the weight of this same stigma by thinking that saving is selfish, that reserves mean you're hoarding, or that donors will judge you for holding too much cash.

But what that Executive Director came to realize, and what I've seen time and time again, is this...

Reserves are not a sign of excess. They're a sign of **endurance.**

Once she began to see reserves not as taking away from her mission, but protecting it, everything changed.

She started small. She reviewed her organization's cash flow, identified where money was just sitting in a checking account, and worked with her board to begin reallocating some of that idle cash into a dedicated reserve.

A year later, that same nonprofit had built a buffer that helped them weather a major program funding delay without laying off staff or cutting services.

Reserves gave the Executive Director and her board more confidence. Flexibility. Time to think strategically instead of scrambling reactively. And it all started by reframing what saving meant.

Because reserves aren't about sitting still, they're about standing strong when it matters most.

The Case for Reserves

If you're still unsure whether your organization can or *should* build reserves, consider this: reserves don't just keep the lights on; they keep the mission alive.

Unforeseen challenges can catch all of us off guard, especially nonprofits. Let's look at a small arts organization and how it pivoted during the COVID-19 pandemic. They had quietly built an operating reserve over the previous few years. They weren't the biggest or best-known nonprofit. They didn't have a million-dollar endowment. But when a crisis hit, they *had a plan.*

While others scrambled to fundraise or cut costs, this organization retained its staff, quickly shifted to virtual programming, and even launched new community initiatives to serve people stuck at home. They weren't reacting — they were ready.

That's what reserves do. They buy you time. They give you options. They allow you to focus on your mission, not just your bank balance.

Now contrast that with another organization: a human services nonprofit that was doing incredibly impactful work in an underserved urban area. They relied heavily on two major fundraising events each year.

When those events were canceled due to the pandemic, their revenue plummeted almost overnight. Without reserves to cushion the blow, they had to furlough staff, pause key programs, and spend months trying to recover lost ground. The community they served felt the impact. So did morale.

Both organizations were mission-driven. Both were led by talented, passionate teams. But only one had the financial foundation to carry its work forward without disruption.

Reserves are not a replacement for fundraising. They're a stabilizing force that enhances your fundraising. When your team isn't panicked about payroll, they can engage donors with confidence and communicate with clarity. Reserves make you more resilient, more strategic, and ultimately more impactful.

These stories highlight one simple truth: reserves change the trajectory of your organization. They're not about sitting on cash; they're about standing on solid ground. Before we go any further, let's clarify what reserves really are, and what they're not.

What Reserves Are and Aren't

A nonprofit reserve fund, also known as **cash reserves** or a rainy-day fund, is essentially your nonprofit's savings account. But unlike operating funds, which are used for day-to-day programmatic costs, e.g., your operating cash flow (OCF), reserve funds are set aside and used sparingly.

Reserves are designated funds for emergencies, such as when expected income falls short or unexpected expenses arise. They aren't "extra" money; they are funds intentionally planned for and set aside for future needs, an unexpected shock, or a strategic opportunity.

Reserves are not a sign of inefficiency or a lack of ambition. They are a sign of strategic foresight and resilience. Here's a quick breakdown:

Cash Reserves Are Not	They Are
✗ A sign that you don't need donations	✓ A safety net in times of uncertainty
✗ A signal that your programs are overfunded	✓ A buffer for cyclical or delayed revenue (like grant payments)
✗ A way to delay important spending decisions indefinitely	✓ A foundation for long-term financial health

Nonprofits are the only sector where having healthy savings is sometimes seen as a negative. Imagine telling a family not to build an emergency savings account because it might make them look rich or advising a business to run with no cash on hand to appear lean. That logic is both flawed and dangerous.

Why Saving *Is* Stewardship

Reserves are mission protection, plain and simple. They aren't just about financial security; they're about safeguarding the impact you've worked so hard to create.

Choosing to build reserves means choosing to protect the mission itself. This ensures that your organization can endure, adapt, and thrive no matter what challenges arise.

Think of it this way: no lasting organization is built on shaky ground. Just as a strong building needs a solid foundation, your nonprofit needs a financial base that can support growth and weather storms. Without it, even the most inspiring mission is at risk. Reserves are that foundation. They allow your organization to evolve confidently, without the looming fear that a downturn or a delayed grant payment might force you to scale back, cut staff, or stop serving.

When you build reserves, you send a clear message to your staff, board, and donors: *We're not just surviving today, we're building something that lasts.* You're not just funding programs; you're laying the groundwork for continued impact for years to come.

From a governance perspective, this is the very definition of fiduciary responsibility. A board that chooses not to establish reserves is not just avoiding tough conversations; it's gambling with the organization's future.

Types of Nonprofit Reserve Funds

Many small and medium-sized nonprofits start with a single reserve fund, but separating funds for different purposes helps with tracking, budgeting, and transparency. There are three main types of reserves you might need:

1. **Operating Reserves**: These funds keep your nonprofit's operations running, such as payroll and routine program costs, during lean times or revenue shortfalls. For example, in today's inflationary environment, nonprofits with healthy operating reserves are better positioned to manage increased costs without jeopardizing their mission.

2. **Capital Reserves**: These funds are set aside for future capital expenses, such as building maintenance, property repairs, or purchasing assets. If you own physical assets, whether it's a building, equipment, or vehicles, you'll need a capital reserve to handle repairs and replacements.

3. **Project Reserves**: Set aside for future projects, such as capital campaigns, large fundraising drives, or multi-year grants. For instance, you might establish a project reserve for a construction project that's planned but won't begin for a couple of years.

The amount of reserves you need will depend on your nonprofit's size, assets, and financial environment. Your goals should be a buffer that covers both expected and unexpected costs, bringing stability to your organization and alleviating stress for your staff and donors.

How Much Should You Save?

There's no perfect formula, but a common best practice is to aim for **six to 12 months of operating expenses in reserves.** (Check out our Appendix for an Operating Cash Flow Expense Calculator).

This gives you the financial runway to weather disruptions, maintain staffing, and adapt without panic. If your organization owns property, you should also plan separately for capital reserves. These funds are dedicated to major repairs or replacements like HVAC systems, roofing, or flooring. These are not part of your operational reserves and must be forecasted independently.

If you find yourself with more than 12 months of operating reserves, that's not a problem; instead, it's an opportunity. You can begin to seed a quasi-endowment (more on this in Chapter 9) or allocate funds toward strategic initiatives and growth. For organizations facing volatile funding cycles or extended grant delays, your reserve target may be even higher.

To guide your planning, start by asking:

- How much of our revenue is predictable?

- What would it cost to operate for 180 days if funding paused?

Remember that we all start at 0. Progress is the goal. Even 90 days of reserves is better than none and already puts you ahead of many organizations living hand-to-mouth. The most important thing is to set a reserve goal and actively work towards it.

As the adage goes, "The best time to plant a tree was 20 years ago. The second-best time is now."

Stewarding Your Reserves Wisely

Where and how you hold your reserves matters. They're not just numbers on a balance sheet — they're a safeguard for your mission's future. With thoughtful stewardship, your reserves can do more than sit idle in a low-interest savings account.

Too often, nonprofits default to parking all reserve funds in checking or savings accounts. While this may feel "safe," it often leaves your funds vulnerable to inflation and limits their growth potential.

Instead, consider strategies that keep your reserves low-risk, highly liquid, and able to generate conservative returns, all while remaining true to your organization's values. Done right, this approach allows your reserves to earn income, strengthen sustainability, and still be readily available when needed.

This is the difference between reactive and proactive financial leadership.

Communicating About Reserves

Worried about donor perception? You're not alone. Many nonprofit leaders feel uneasy about showing reserve balances in public disclosures or donor conversations. But the truth is, when communicated clearly and confidently, reserves are a sign of thoughtful stewardship, and most donors respect that.

Consider framing it this way:

- "We maintain a six-month reserve to ensure we can serve our community, even during uncertain times."

- "We created a reserve policy so we never have to cut programs and can ensure long-term, even generational, impact on our mission."

- "This reserve is part of our strategic plan to grow sustainably and invest in innovation."

When you own the narrative around your reserves, you invite donors into your long-term vision and demonstrate the leadership required to sustain it.

Best Practices for Managing Your Operating Reserves

To put your reserve strategy into action, start with these steps:

- **Keep your operating budget separate** – use a checking or high-yield savings account for day-to-day expenses. Don't confuse your operating cash flow (OCF) with your reserves.

- **Segment your reserves** – create separate Operating, Capital, and Project reserve accounts to increase transparency and accountability.

- **Partner with a nonprofit-savvy advisor** – they'll help you manage cash efficiently and avoid bank limitations that weren't designed for tax-exempt entities.

- **Invest wisely** – consider starting with low-risk, highly liquid options such as Treasury bills, money market mutual funds, or other fixed income. We explore this more in Chapter 8, "Growing with Guardrails".

- **Allocate additional funds with purpose** – use surplus dollars to fund new initiatives, support innovation, or seed a quasi-endowment for long-term strength.

The Bigger Payoff: Transparency, Sustainability, Trust

Effective cash management brings powerful benefits:

- **Greater financial clarity** – with clear tracking and policies, you'll gain sharper insights into your financial health and make better decisions as a result

- **Increased sustainability** – conservative returns from properly invested reserves add another layer of stability to your funding strategy

- **Stronger donor relationships** – donors trust organizations that manage their funds wisely. Transparency and foresight inspire loyalty, plus unlock larger, longer-term gifts

Building a reserve fund is only the beginning. With proper stewardship and cash reserve management, your nonprofit can grow its operating reserves and ultimately achieve more for your mission.

The Leadership to Build for Tomorrow

When you choose to build reserves, you're choosing to lead with courage and vision. You're telling your team, your board, and your community: "We're not here just to survive. We're here to endure."

Reserves protect your mission, empower your planning, and give you the freedom to grow with confidence. They're not a sign of excess. They're a sign of leadership.

A Final Story to Carry Forward

One Executive Director told me, "We used to hold our breath every April, hoping we could make payroll before our big fundraiser in June." After they built just three months of operating reserves, she said it changed everything: "Now, I sleep at night. I have the freedom to think beyond the crisis in front of me."

That's what reserves give you, not just cash in the bank, but confidence in the future.

It struck me how closely this mirrors the very people many nonprofits exist to serve. A food-insecure family can't focus on career goals or education when they're worried about their next meal.

Survival mode crowds out higher-level thinking. In the same way, a nonprofit in financial scarcity can't think about growth, innovation, or long-term impact. All of its energy is spent on the next payroll, the next grant cycle, the next urgent appeal.

One organization I worked with eventually named this irony out loud: "We're fighting to end the very cycle we're trapped in." That realization was the turning point. By building reserves, they created the same stability for their mission that they were working so hard to create for their community.

In the next chapter, we'll explore how to translate that confidence into strategy, bringing clarity, buy-in, and alignment to your leadership team and board. Because reserves alone don't build trust: how you manage and communicate them does.

Key Takeaways for Your Mission

- **Saving Is Smart Stewardship**
  Reserves are not hoarding; they're the foundation of long-term impact.

- **Reserves Give You Options, Not Excuses**
  With margin, you can be proactive, not reactive.

- **One Size Doesn't Fit All**
  Your reserve strategy should reflect your reality and needs. Start where you are and grow.

- **Communicate with Confidence**
  Don't hide your reserves from your board, donors, or team, but explain them as part of your strategic vision for mission sustainability.

- **Make Your Money Work for You**
  Wise stewardship means finding the balance, growing your reserves thoughtfully while keeping them lower risk, liquid, and ready to serve your mission at any time.

CHAPTER 5

How to Move Beyond the Bank

For many nonprofits, the bank is where the relationship with money begins and, too often, where it stays. It's where donations are received, where payroll is run, and where board treasurers glance at monthly statements to see if things look "normal." There's comfort in that routine. Banks feel familiar, safe, and steady.

But over time, familiarity can become a limitation. Especially when your nonprofit starts to build reserves, receives a major gift, or accumulates more cash than it immediately needs for operations. In those moments, continuing to rely on traditional bank accounts for longer-term financial needs can hold your organization back from real sustainability.

This chapter is about reimagining that relationship. We're not talking about replacing your bank but complementing it with a strategy that allows your mission to grow. It's time to move from mere safekeeping to thoughtful, strategic stewardship.

Why Banks Weren't Built for You (And Why That's Okay)

To understand why many nonprofits feel stuck financially, it helps to look backward. The U.S. banking system was created in the 1800s, long before the concept of a "tax-exempt entity" even existed. From the beginning, banks were designed to serve two audiences: individual consumers and for-profit businesses. Nonprofits weren't part of the equation, and it shows.

While many modern banks are eager to support nonprofit clients, the systems they operate in still reflect those origins. Account structures, onboarding requirements, and risk assessments are all optimized for corporate or personal banking. When a nonprofit applies, the process often feels incredibly difficult, and it's not because banks don't care, but because your needs simply fall outside the norm.

Navigating tax-exempt status, rotating volunteer board members, mission-restricted funds, and multiple stakeholder layers introduces a level of complexity that most traditional banking systems weren't built to accommodate. Banks often struggle with the Know Your Customer (KYC) and Anti-

Money Laundering (AML) compliance when it comes to nonprofits. And when your organization has frequent leadership turnover or nuanced programmatic spending restrictions, it only complicates things further.

The result? Many banks offer you the basics (checking, savings, maybe a CD) but not much else. And while they're essential for day-to-day operations, many are simply not structured to help nonprofits grow long-term financial strength.

That's not a reason to abandon your banking partners. It's a reason to expand your tools.

When "Safe" Stops Being Smart

Let's talk about what feels safe. For most nonprofit boards, the safest place for money typically feels like the bank. And for short-term needs (payroll, rent, programming) that's exactly right.

But what about the rest? The reserves you're not planning to touch for six months or more? The unrestricted gifts that don't have an immediate use? The campaign surplus is sitting untouched? If those dollars are sitting in a low-interest checking or savings account, they're quietly losing value every day.

Inflation doesn't care that your money is "safe." If inflation is running at 2%–3% and your bank account is earning 0.8%, your buying power is shrinking. Slowly, quietly, but steadily.

It's like trying to fill a bucket with a leak at the bottom. You don't see it right away, but over time, you're left with less.

And there's another kind of risk: insurance limits. FDIC coverage only protects up to $250,000 per entity per bank (not per account). Many nonprofits, especially those with healthy reserves, regularly exceed that limit. To stay within insured thresholds, organizations often open multiple accounts at different banks, creating administrative headaches and complexity for already-stretched teams. The more "safe" accounts you open, the harder it becomes to manage the whole picture.

Worse yet is the opportunity cost. Every dollar that's left idle could potentially be earning 3%–5% or more in a conservative investment strategy. Over time, that adds up – into salaries funded, programs expanded, and missions advanced.

Safety is not the absence of risk. It's the presence of a plan.

Reframing Risk: A Stewardship Mindset

Risk is often misunderstood in the nonprofit space. Leaders tend to think of it as something to be avoided or something that belongs in the realm of Wall Street, not mission-driven organizations.

But in reality, not all risk is created equal. Some risk is reckless. Some is measured. And some risk, when wisely managed, becomes opportunity.

Putting money under your mattress may feel secure, but even those funds would risk loss from theft, fire, or inflation. Leaving money in a checking account may feel conservative, but it's actually exposed to inflation and underperformance. Even CDs, which lock up cash for a fixed rate, lack liquidity and can return less than current inflation depending on the duration, guaranteeing a net loss in real value.

Wise risk is something else entirely. Stewardship is choosing where and how to invest your resources in a way that aligns with your time horizon, your mission, and your liquidity needs. It does take courage and conviction to ask, *"We may not need these funds for two years, so how can we put them to work until then?"* It's not risky to ask that question. It's responsible.

Shifting Gears: Moving from Idle Cash to Strategic Reserves

Shifting your strategy doesn't mean walking away from your bank. It means using the bank for what it does best, handling daily cash flow, and then partnering with professionals who specialize in managing longer-term reserves.

For example, if your organization has more than six months of operating expenses in the bank or recently received a large unrestricted gift with no immediate need, that's a signal it's time to explore more strategic options.

A brokerage account can give you access to a broader set of tools: higher-yield savings, money market funds, treasury bills, and conservative bond portfolios, all of which are liquid, transparent, and aligned with nonprofit values.

Many brokerage platforms also offer **FDIC sweep programs**, which automatically allocate cash across a network of partner banks behind the scenes. This can often give your organization access to up to millions of dollars in FDIC insurance coverage, without the hassle of managing dozens of accounts. Everything stays under one roof, with one login and one statement. Your finance committee and team will thank you.

In practical terms, this means fewer accounts to manage, better visibility, stronger yields, and peace of mind.

For some leaders, this all clicks immediately. For others, it can feel overwhelming. That's understandable, but it doesn't make it less important. With every great mission comes the responsibility to steward resources wisely. You stepped into this work because you care deeply about impact, and financial strategy is inseparable from that calling.

Healthy stewardship is honoring donors, protecting your team, and ensuring your mission endures. When you connect thoughtful financial management to donor trust, you unlock the very fuel that makes your programs possible.

This isn't a distraction from your mission; it's the practical expression of it.

When to Consider Moving Beyond the Bank

Here are clear signs it's time to explore a brokerage or advisory relationship for part of your funds:

- You're holding **more than six months of operating expenses** in a checking or savings account.

- Your board has approved the creation of **a reserve fund or quasi-endowment**.

- You're receiving **one-time gifts, stocks, bequests, Charitable Lead Annuity Trust, Charitable Remainder Unitrust, life insurance, annuity, or campaign surpluses,** and don't have an immediate use for the funds.

- You want to consolidate multiple accounts across banks for simplicity and clarity.

- You have more in an account than the **FDIC's $250,000 limit** and are concerned about coverage gaps.

- You are receiving grants you don't need to buy down right away

It's not an all-or-nothing shift. You can keep your operational accounts at the bank and move reserve funds to a brokerage. Use the bank for daily liquidity, and use a trusted advisor for strategy, growth, and protection.

A New Approach to Cash and Purpose

One of the most powerful mindset shifts a nonprofit can make is to align cash management with purpose and timing. Instead of asking, "How much do we have in the bank?" start asking, "When will we need this money – and what is it meant to do?"

Short-term operating cash should absolutely stay at the bank because that's your runway for the next 30, 60, 90 days. But funds that won't be used for six months to a year? Those can be placed in high-yield money markets or short-term Treasuries. Reserves that won't be needed for a few years, such as for capital improvements or strategic expansion, can be placed in a conservative fixed income strategy with slightly more yield and time to grow.

Even longer-term funds, such as quasi-endowments or major campaign reserves, can be placed in a blended portfolio that balances growth and stability while staying aligned with your Investment Policy Statement (IPS). The key is matching the timeline of the money to the right financial strategy.

This doesn't have to be complex. But it does need to be intentional.

Making the Move: What to Expect

When you decide to move from banking-only to a more comprehensive financial strategy, it's natural to have questions. What will the process look like? Who's responsible for oversight? What does transparency look like?

The good news is, with the right advisor, this shift should feel familiar and easy. You'll still have easy access to your funds. You'll receive clear statements and quarterly board reports. What's even better is that you'll now have support from a fiduciary whose job is to act in your best interest, not sell products.

More importantly, you'll gain a partner who can help you build a financial strategy rooted in your mission, one who can draft your IPS, meet with your board, answer questions, and help guide decisions that honor your values and vision.

Partnering with Both Your Bank and Advisor

This isn't about picking sides but truly thinking about the roles your partners are best suited for.

Banks remain essential for operations. They're the backbone of cash flow, bill pay, and payroll. They process credit card donations, issue debit cards, and keep the day-to-day running.

Advisors, on the other hand, bring a different kind of support. They help you craft long-term financial strategies.

They manage risk and allocation. They help you invest reserves, protect purchasing power, and build growth, all while maintaining mission alignment and fiduciary responsibility.

When banks and advisors are each doing what they do best, your nonprofit wins. You gain operational confidence, clarity, and strategic capacity. And most importantly, you can focus on your mission and do more good.

The Hidden Cost of Waiting

One of the biggest threats to nonprofit financial health is not bad decision-making — it's indecision. Money sitting idle isn't just stagnant, it's potentially shrinking. Here's another example of what this can look like in real life...

Consider a nonprofit with $500,000 in reserves, sitting in a checking or savings account earning 0.1%. After one year, that balance grows by just $500. But place that same money in a conservative, liquid strategy earning 4.5%, and you've earned over $22,000 in one year.

Over five years, that difference could fund an entirely new staff position or provide emergency support during a funding shortfall.

The cost of waiting isn't always visible on the balance sheet. But it shows up in the missed opportunities, the programs that didn't launch, and the pressure to fundraise more instead of making better use of what you already have. If you can move from a scarcity mindset into a longer-term strategy mindset, then that is what sets the table for sustainability.

Moving from Comfort to Clarity

Shifting from safekeeping to strategic growth doesn't mean abandoning what you know. It means expanding what's possible. It means realizing that what feels "safe" isn't always what's best, and that the best decisions are ones made with clarity, confidence, and intention.

Start by reviewing your current accounts. Talk to your board. Name what money is for today, what's for tomorrow, and what's for the future. Then take action, one step at a time.

Because when your money is working as hard as your mission, **that's financial stewardship.**

And that's the path to long-term, sustainable impact.

From Cautious to Confident – How One Nonprofit Reclaimed Its Financial Momentum

When a mid-sized nonprofit focused on housing and community development received a surprise $400,000 bequest from a longtime donor, the executive director, Leah, was both thrilled and cautious. She knew this was a rare and potentially transformative gift, one that could provide long-needed stability to their work if they were careful. But she also knew her board had a long history of playing it safe when it came to finances.

"We've never had this much in the bank," one board member said. "Let's just park it in our savings account until we figure out what to do."

So that's what they did.

Six months later, Leah ran the numbers. The money had earned very little in interest. At the same time, inflation was ticking upward, and their program expenses were increasing. She brought the issue to the Board.

"We're losing value by doing nothing," she said. "It may feel like we're protecting the gift, but in reality, we're letting it shrink."

There was hesitation. Words like "risk" and "volatility" surfaced immediately. Some board members feared criticism for doing anything that seemed too financial or "Wall Street." But Leah framed the conversation differently.

"What if we treated this gift not as something to protect from change, but something to protect for impact? What if we grew it slowly, intentionally, in a way that actually extended the donor's legacy?"

That reframing shifted the tone. The board agreed to meet with a nonprofit-focused advisor who helped them draft a simple Investment Policy Statement, define their reserve strategy, and open a brokerage account with a conservative allocation to government bonds and a high-yield sweep program.

That year, the gift generated more than $17,000 in additional income, without touching the principal.

Today, the nonprofit uses that annual interest income to support emergency rental assistance and rapid rehousing efforts in neighborhoods that used to be left waiting on grant cycles. The gift didn't just sit in the bank. It grew. It provided margin. And most importantly, it fueled the mission for years to come.

Looking back, Leah reflected, "We just needed to stop being afraid of growth. We still love our bank, and we use it every day. But now we use it for what it does best, and we have another experienced fiduciary partner who helped us establish a legacy fund for what it's meant to do: move our mission forward for decades to come."

Key Takeaways for Your Mission

- **Banks Are for Operations, Not Strategy**
  Banks are essential for day-to-day cash flow, but they weren't designed with nonprofit needs in mind and offer limited tools for long-term financial growth. Relying on banks alone can limit sustainability.

- **Playing It "Safe" Can Be Costly**
  Keeping reserves in low-interest accounts exposes nonprofits to inflation, coverage gaps, and lost opportunity. What feels safe may actually erode your purchasing power and mission capacity.

- **Strategic Risk = Responsible Stewardship**
  Risk isn't just something to avoid. When managed wisely, an investment portfolio with a range of risks is a tool for growth. Investing reserves based on timing, risk tolerance, and purpose is not reckless; it's responsible financial leadership.

- **Growth Starts with Intention**
  Moving beyond the bank doesn't require millions or complex strategies. With a clear plan, nonprofits can align their cash with purpose, simplify oversight, and scale their impact without abandoning financial caution.

CHAPTER 6

Translating Cash to Confidence: Your Tiered Financial Strategy

Y ou've done the hard work of building reserves. Now what?

It's time to put that foundation to work. This chapter is about turning financial preparedness into a strategy, transforming idle cash into mission-aligned momentum. Because having money in the bank isn't the finish line; actually, it's the starting line. The true goal is not only to preserve your mission but, more importantly, to propel it forward.

In this next section, we'll guide you through building a tiered investment strategy for your nonprofit that gives your team clarity, your board confidence, and your organization the ability to grow with intention. By segmenting your reserves into Short-, Mid-, and Long-term strategies, every dollar gains a defined purpose and every decision becomes easier.

We aren't just chasing returns. We are stewarding what you've been entrusted with wisely, clearly, and courageously.

Defining Your Financial Horizons

Without clear segmentation, nonprofit funds often end up in one general account sitting idle, unassigned, and underperforming. This creates confusion for stakeholders, fuels reactive decisions, and limits your ability to plan with confidence.

The solution? Define your financial horizons.

Think of your funds in distinct categories, each with a clear purpose and time frame:

- **Short-term (0–12 months)** – Operating budget, emergency reserves, and grant funds

- **Mid-term (1–3 years)** – Growth initiatives, longer-term reserves, and capital campaigns

- **Long-term (3+ years)** – Endowments, legacy giving, and strategic expansion

This framework is more than just labeling accounts; it's a mindset shift. By assigning every dollar a specific role and purpose, you ensure the right funds are always available at the right time. Operational dollars remain safe and accessible, while long-term dollars can be invested more strategically for growth.

When your board and leadership team can see exactly what's protected for tomorrow versus what's positioned for the future, decision-making becomes faster and the fear of risk decreases. You're not gambling, you're stair-stepping your risk thoughtfully, taking small, measured risks only on funds with the longest time horizons.

Here's why it works:

- **Protects immediate needs:** Short-term funds are liquid and ready for daily operations

- **Removes "use it or lose it" pressure:** Designations protect funds from being spent impulsively

- **Streamlines decisions:** Clear categories reduce debate and delay

- **Builds trust:** A transparent, time-bound plan shows stakeholders you're leading with strategy, not chance

A Quick Example:

One nonprofit I worked with had one general bucket of funds with $750,000 just sitting in a checking account. It felt "safe," but it wasn't working for them. After defining their financial horizons and reconsidering their purpose, they structured their reserves into:

- $250,000 as Short-term reserves for operations

- $200,000 into a Mid-term fixed income strategy for a planned facility upgrade

- $300,000 into a Long-term investment fund for scholarships and endowment growth

The result? They could still pay every bill on time from their operating cash flow, but they also watched their Mid- and Long-term funds grow with higher yields and compound interest without touching their Short-term stability.

When a major donor visited later that year, they could clearly show how each dollar was positioned for impact and sustainability, which inspired an additional six-figure gift.

By defining your financial horizons, you transform a lump sum of "cash in the bank" into a clear, confident strategy for sustainability and growth.

Short-Term: The Bedrock of Financial Stability

Your short-term strategy is not only about your operating budget, but it's also about your reserves. This bucket includes both the cash you need to meet regular monthly obligations and the additional funds set aside to cover unexpected disruptions, like a delayed grant payment or urgent repairs.

Think of it in two parts:

- **Operating cash flow (OCF)**: lives in your checking or savings account. Your OCF covers your day-to-day budget: payroll, rent, and vendor payments. Most nonprofits should keep roughly three to six months of rolling operating in their checking account.

- **Short-term operating reserves**: These are your safety net. Ideally, six months to a year of operating expenses that is held in a separate brokerage account in low-risk and highly liquid holdings. This allows you the opportunity to earn more than traditional savings accounts.

Your goal here is simple: *accessibility without sacrificing opportunity*. You want your emergency funds to be available within a few days, not tied up in long-term vehicles, but you also want them to grow modestly rather than sit idle in a bank account earning little interest.

Recommended tools for Short-term reserves:

Your Short-term reserves should be safe, liquid, and working for you – not just sitting idle. Your Financial Advisor can help make the right recommendation for you, but here are common tools to consider:

- **Money Market Mutual Funds** – Offer strong liquidity and typically yield more than standard bank money market accounts, while maintaining low risk.

- **Treasury Bills (T-Bills)** – Government-backed, highly secure, and a trusted option for preserving short-term funds.

- **Diversified Fixed Income** – Depending on market conditions, short-duration bonds or other fixed income strategies can target higher yields without taking on excessive risk.

- **Certificates of Deposit (CDs)** – A traditional option for nonprofits, but use caution. CDs limit liquidity and often have penalties for early withdrawal. If using CDs, consider *laddering* (staggering maturity dates) and, for larger deposits, using **CDARS** to increase FDIC coverage.

- **Sweep Programs via Brokerage** – Some financial partners (like Infinite Giving) offer FDIC sweep programs that automatically spread your funds across a network of banks. This means your money continues to earn interest while remaining fully liquid and accessible.

The real advantage? Instead of being limited to just $250,000 of FDIC insurance at a single bank, your funds are divided into multiple accounts behind the scenes, dramatically increasing your total insured coverage.

For nonprofits, this means stronger protection, better yields, and less administrative hassle compared to managing multiple separate bank relationships on your own.

How an Animal Shelter Made Its Savings Work Harder

A mid-sized animal welfare nonprofit kept all of their funds (both operating cash and reserves) in a traditional bank savings account at below 1% APY. They had the right instincts to save, but their reserves were barely earning interest.

By moving those short-term reserves into money market mutual funds through a brokerage account, they were able to target over 4% APY, generating returns that helped cover rising veterinary and food costs.

Same dollars. Greater impact.

This kind of short-term strategy builds both stability and momentum. It ensures your day-to-day needs are protected while allowing your reserves to actively support your mission rather than sitting idle on the sidelines.

Mid-Term: Flexibility for Growth

Once your short-term needs are secure, it's time to look a bit further ahead. What strategic initiatives are on your horizon? Are you preparing for a renovation, launching a new program, upgrading technology, or planning for a multi-year grant cycle? These 1–3-year goals deserve a place in your tiered financial strategy.

Mid-term funds should strike a careful balance: accessible enough to use when the time comes, but positioned for more growth potential than Short-term reserves. Depending on time horizons and risk tolerance, this could include longer-term reserves, operational reserves over six months, multi-year capital campaigns or grants, and much more.

Recommended tools:

- **Bond Funds:** Municipal or high-quality corporate bonds for predictable, relatively safe returns.

- **Dividend-Paying Stocks:** Blue-chip companies with steady payouts for income you can reinvest or deploy when needed.

- **Certificate of Deposit Account Registry Service (CDARS):** This allows a nonprofit to place a large deposit with one Advisor but have it automatically divided into smaller CDs (Certificates of Deposit) at multiple banks within a network. Each CD is kept under the $250,000 FDIC insurance limit, so the entire deposit remains fully insured.

- **Fixed Income Portfolios:** Professionally managed mixes of bonds such as U.S. Treasuries, municipal bonds, and high-quality corporate debt that are designed to provide steady income and preserve capital. Choosing a portfolio rather than hand-picking individual bonds provides nonprofits with diversification, risk management, and ongoing oversight without the burden of managing each investment on their own.

How a Community Mental Health Center Funded Their Next Big Leap

A community mental health center had a two-year plan to expand its counseling services and open a new satellite clinic. Rather than letting the earmarked funds sit in a low-yield savings account, they moved them into a mid-term portfolio of intermediate bond funds and dividend-paying stocks. The dividends were reinvested, steadily growing the balance, while the bond allocation preserved stability.

When the lease was signed and construction began, their investment gains helped cover increased build-out and equipment costs, without needing to launch an emergency fundraising appeal.

Same dollars. Greater impact.

Mid-term planning provides something every nonprofit needs but often lacks: flexibility. And flexibility is what allows your mission to adapt, grow, and lead.

Long-Term: Growing Your Mission with Impact

Long-term investments are designed to be your biggest vision for the future you're building and not just for next year, but for the next generation. These funds often fuel endowments, board-designated reserves, or strategic initiatives that won't need to be accessed for the next five to 10 years or more.

At this stage, your strategy shifts from preservation to growth. Not speculation, but disciplined, diversified investing designed to outpace inflation, generate income, and expand your mission's reach over time.

Recommended tools:

- **Diversified Equity Funds:** Broad-market or global equity strategies for long-term growth and inflation protection.

- **Balanced Portfolios:** A mix of stocks, bonds, and alternatives to provide steady returns while managing volatility. A benefit to these diversified portfolios is that they are curated to target higher returns within a lower risk profile.

Another topic to consider is active vs. passive management. Passive management is often a better fit for nonprofits because it prioritizes low cost, transparency, and long-term consistency. Studies show that over 10 years more than 85% of actively managed funds underperform their passive benchmarks after fees *(S&P SPIVA U.S. Scorecard, 2023)*. For nonprofits, this means that more passive strategies allow more donor dollars to stay focused on mission impact.

How a Human Services Nonprofit Built a Legacy

A Human Services Nonprofit wanted to create a permanent funding stream for local grants. They started with a $1 million endowment and, with a long-term horizon, built a diversified portfolio blending equities for growth and fixed income for stability. Over 10 years, the principal grew to nearly $1.5 million while still producing an average of $50,000+ annually in dependable income.

That growth meant 100 more families were supported, without increasing fundraising pressure on their donors.

Same dollars. Greater impact.

Long-term investing allows your mission to outlast your annual budget. You don't need to pick stocks and time the market (please don't). You need a tiered investment strategy customized to each bucket of funds to align purpose, goals, and timelines. Long-term investing builds legacy, and legacy is what changes the world.

Stewarding Donor Funds Thoughtfully

Nonprofit funds are donor funds, given in trust and entrusted to your care. That's both an honor and a responsibility. Stewardship isn't just about keeping the lights on today but ensuring those dollars create lasting impact tomorrow.

Thoughtful stewardship must be intentional, not reactive. Letting reserves sit idle in low-yield accounts quietly costs your mission every year through lost opportunity and inflation. The true risk isn't in investing wisely; it's in doing nothing and watching purchasing power fade.

Imagine if the Ford Foundation had never invested. Founded in 1936 by Edsel and Henry Ford, it started with a seed gift of about $25,000. Fast forward nearly 90 years, and its endowment was reported at $16 billion in its 2023 tax filings*.

The vast majority of that expansion comes from investment returns, compounding over decades. Similarly, the Carnegie Corporation of New York was established in 1911 with around $125 million in initial funding from Andrew Carnegie. As of 2024 tax filings, its total assets sit between $4–5 billion.

*Note – most nonprofits' IRS Form 990 data is on ProPublica.com

That financial growth is almost entirely due to the power of compounding interest building over time, reinvesting earnings, and staying patient. The same principle applies to your organization: what feels like a modest investment today can transform into something powerful decades down the line. You just have to think long-term.

Strategic investing isn't about speculation or chasing big returns. With thoughtful stewardship, you're giving every dollar a job, stretching donor contributions further, and protecting your mission against uncertainty. That's how you honor the trust placed in you.

And the good news is you don't have to figure it out alone. In fact, you shouldn't. Managing these resources well means finding the right partners who understand the unique financial realities of nonprofits and can help you steward donor dollars with both wisdom and purpose.

The Importance of Partnering with Experts

As a nonprofit leader, you already wear a dozen hats. "Financial strategist" shouldn't have to be one of them.

Yes, your board likely includes experienced bankers or investment professionals, and their insight is valuable. But nonprofit finance is different: different brokerage requirements, reserve policy governance, tax-exempt restrictions, and donor-intent considerations. Even seasoned financial professionals often need guidance tailored to the nonprofit context.

That's why the best approach is to partner with a nonprofit-specific fiduciary who works alongside your leadership. Someone who understands your mission, your compliance requirements, and your culture, not just your balance sheet.

At Infinite Giving, we built our advisory model specifically for this role: combining nonprofit leadership experience with cash management, policy, and investment expertise so your dollars are both protected and productive. Whether you work with us or another qualified fiduciary, the goal is the same: ensure your resources are managed with clarity, transparency, and an unwavering commitment to your mission.

And remember, **your financially skilled board members shouldn't be the ones directly managing your investments.** While their expertise is valuable, having them run accounts creates real risks. Board members rotate off after a few years, and with term limits in place, continuity is quickly lost. Even more concerning, when board members manage investments themselves, it opens the door to conflicts of interest. There's also an increased risk of working in conflict of good governance.

Their true role is far more important: to help you select the right advisor, ask the right questions, and hold that advisor accountable. That way, your leadership team can focus on stewarding the mission, while your board fulfills its responsibility to oversee (not operate) your financial strategy.

The Confidence to Grow

Translating your cash into confidence is about having a plan and the right partners. As a reminder, this is why a tiered investment strategy helps you:

- ✔ Keep your daily operations stable in **Short-term** reserves
- ✔ Invest in **Mid-term** opportunities
- ✔ Build **Long-term** sustainability
- ✔ Communicate your vision with clarity and credibility
- ✔ Increase transparency and accountability

And ultimately, it also builds confidence and trust with your board, with your donors, and with your team.

All nonprofit leaders should be able to operate from a place of financial confidence. You need a strategy that's aligned, understandable, and adaptable. You need trusted voices at the table. And above all, you need the courage to steward well.

Your financial strategy is not separate from your mission; it's the structure that supports it. When your cash is organized, your confidence grows. And when your confidence grows, so does your impact.

Key Takeaways for Your Mission

- **Tiered Investing Turns Cash into Strategy**
  Simply having reserves isn't enough. By segmenting your funds into Short-, Mid-, and Long-term tiers, and clearly defining each fund's purpose, you align financial decisions with your mission and help your team move from reactive to proactive.

- **Defined Financial Horizons Build Clarity and Trust**
  Categorizing funds by purpose and time horizon protects immediate needs, prevents the pressure to overspend, and boosts decision-making and transparency with staff, boards, and donors.

- **Mission-aligned Growth Doesn't Require High Risk**
  Strategic tools, such as money market funds, bonds, and diversified portfolios, offer conservative growth tailored to nonprofits' unique needs by helping to preserve access and potentially generate meaningful returns.

- **You Don't Have to Do This Alone**
  Partnering with nonprofit-specific financial experts ensures your investment strategy is compliant, mission-focused, and built to navigate the sector's unique barriers. This allows you to focus on impact, not just income.

CHAPTER 7

From Plan to Practice: Aligning People and Policy

You've done the hard work of defining your tiered financial strategy. You've categorized your funds and mapped out what Short-Term, Mid-Term, and Long-Term sustainability looks like for your organization. Now comes the part where many nonprofits stumble, and it's not in planning, but in practice.

This chapter is about what happens next to make your strategy a reality. We're putting structure behind your financial goals, building buy-in, and creating a culture where your strategy actually lives, not just in board minutes, but in day-to-day decisions.

Because the truth is: a strategy only works when your people are aligned. When your board understands what you're building. When your staff knows how their work contributes to sustainability. And when everyone is rowing in the same direction, confident that your organization is prepared for the future.

We're moving from financial theory to financial trust. From ideas to execution. These core tenets will help you get from plan to practice:

1. Develop an Investment Policy Statement (IPS) to move from fear to strategy

2. Choose a fiduciary partner and advisory firm that specializes in nonprofits

3. Make transparency routine by sharing regular updates with your board, team, and even major donors

Financial Clarity Starts with Cultural Alignment

When we talk about financial strategy, it's easy to focus on balance sheets, reserve targets, and investment policies. But at the heart of it all is something more human: trust.

Trust that your leadership is making smart decisions. Trust that your board is stewarding resources well. Trust that the mission will still be thriving years from now.

That kind of trust doesn't come from numbers alone. It comes from clarity. It comes from a shared language. And it comes from a team that understands not just *what* you're doing with your money but *why*.

When your board, leadership, and staff all see your financial strategy as a mission strategy, they'll feel empowered to support it. That's cultural alignment, and it's one of the most overlooked but powerful tools for nonprofit financial sustainability.

Engaging Your Board as Financial Stewards

Many nonprofit leaders feel frustrated when they can't get their board to act confidently on financial matters. But here's the real challenge: it's not that board members don't care; sometimes it's that they don't always know *how* to engage.

Most board members join because they're passionate about the mission, not because they're nonprofit experts. Many come from the business world and bring strong financial skills, but even then, for-profit logic doesn't always translate to nonprofit realities. Donor money feels different, and it is!

The result? Well-intentioned hesitation. Boards become overly cautious. They keep too much money in checking "just in case." They delay investment decisions. They worry about what donors will think or what the proper next step to take is.

This is where your leadership matters most. Your role is not to force decisions; it's to create clarity. When board members understand how reserves protect programs, or how an IPS guides growth responsibly, **they shift from fear to strategy.**

And remember: the board's role is governance, not financial management. They oversee Advisors; they don't invest the funds themselves. With rolling board terms, volunteer status, and conflicts of interest, this can get messy fast. Board members are stewards, not CFOs. Expecting them to carry out the day-to-day strategy is not only unrealistic, but it can also lead to burnout or blurred boundaries.

What they can do is set strong policies, ask the right questions, and ensure that financial decisions align with your mission. That's powerful stewardship.

From Confusion to Clarity

Here's another real-life example. When a new executive director stepped into a passionate, people-first organization, she quickly discovered a deeply cautious board. They had been burned by a funding cut years prior and some past board mismanagement, and in response, locked down the budget. Every dollar was scrutinized. Any talk of investing reserves was met with worry, which was understandable.

But this meant that the organization had six months of cash that was earning nothing because it was sitting in a low-interest savings account. And, the board didn't want to move it. *"What if something happens?"* they asked.

The executive director understood their fear, but she also saw the cost. They were losing thousands each year in potential earnings, and worse, the hesitation was stalling innovation. New program ideas were shelved. Strategic hiring was postponed.

So, she took a different approach.

First, she reframed the conversation. Instead of presenting spreadsheets and return assumptions, she told the story of what stability could unlock. "If we earn even 3% annually on our reserves," she explained, "that's enough to fund our summer mentorship program without asking donors for another dollar."

Then she introduced an IPS that outlined their tiered financial strategy, complete with goals, risk tolerance, spending guardrails, and decision-making structure. The board didn't need to become experts; they just needed a clear, mission-aligned roadmap.

By the end of the year, they had adopted the IPS, moved part of their reserves into a conservative brokerage account, and began quarterly reviews with their finance committee. Confidence grew.

You see, the board needed to have the confidence that the investments were being stewarded well. They had defined their risk tolerance together and partnered with someone who understood their unique needs and curated strategies accordingly. That transparency and clarity were vital to growing their trust and confidence.

Within 18 months, the organization launched a new peer counseling initiative funded entirely through investment income. The board shifted from saying, *"We can't afford it!"* to asking, *"How can we fund this strategically?"*

The executive director not only built a strategy; she built alignment. And it changed everything for the better.

Creating Structure that Builds Confidence

Your board doesn't need to master every investment term or accounting rule. What they need is a roadmap.

That's where a well-crafted IPS comes in.

An IPS is more than a document — it's a commitment. It outlines how your organization approaches risk, spending, and growth. It clarifies who is responsible for what and when decisions should be reviewed. It brings structure to discussions that often feel ambiguous.

Most importantly, an IPS shows that you're thinking long-term. It gives your board the confidence to act, not just react. And it helps shift your culture from fear-based financial decision-making to values-driven planning.

(We've even included an IPS template in the Appendix of this book to help get you started)

The IPS doesn't require a million-dollar endowment to be useful. In fact, most organizations start small by setting basic guardrails, then building over time (we talk about this more in the next chapter). Remember that the best practice for getting started at a high level looks like this:

- **Short-term** by creating or designating your cash reserve funds

- **Mid-term** investments for growth and capital campaigns

- Eventually, **Long-term** legacy gifts such as endowments.

This is how financial maturity grows: not with one big leap, but through steady, aligned action.

From Strategy to Shared Vision

An effective financial strategy should be both practical and inspiring. It needs to be actionable, yes, but also something your people can believe in.

Here are 5 steps on how to bring that strategy to life, and remind us all that you don't need to have a massive endowment to generate dividends that fund your mission:

1. Lead with Clarity

Skip the jargon. Use plain language to connect the numbers to the mission. *"Why are you building reserves?"* So we never have to cut staff or services during a funding gap. *"Why invest long-term?"* So we can serve more people, for longer. Clarity invites confidence. Use visuals, analogies, and impact stories to bring your financial strategy to life.

2. Set Guardrails

Every good strategy needs boundaries. Start with basic policies such as:

- "We maintain six months of operating cash."

- "Reserves are board-approved only for emergencies or strategic growth."

- "We review our investment allocation quarterly."

Then build toward a formal IPS. Guardrails aren't in place to limit your growth, but they're designed to protect your organization on your journey to sustainability.

3. Identify Risk Honestly

Financial maturity doesn't mean pretending everything's fine. It means naming your risks and planning ahead.

- What happens if a major grant falls through?

- What if inflation drives up your costs?

- What if the giving trends shift?

Donors and board members alike will respect that you're not just building for good times but you're preparing for whatever circumstances your organization will face.

4. Communicate in Mission Terms

People don't get excited about liquidity ratios. They get excited about the work. Think about the story you can tell about how you made your cash have a greater impact on your organization. And make sure to keep it in simple, plain language, such as:

- "With reserves, we can make sure our food pantry stays open so no one goes hungry during the worst of times."

- "Our investment income helps cover summer program costs every year."

Always remember: mission outcomes are your most powerful financial narrative.

5. Make Transparency Routine

Don't wait for crises to communicate. Share regular updates with your board, team, and even major donors. Use dashboards and data visualizations to make it easy to understand.

Transparency creates engagement. When people are fully aware of what's going on, they're more likely to support the plan and the person leading it.

The Real Payoff: Confidence and Culture

Financial strategy is not only about money; it's also about leadership. When you lead with transparency and trust, your board follows. When your policies are clear and values-aligned, your team feels secure.

Over time, this builds a culture that isn't afraid to discuss financial strategy. A culture that knows reserves are a sign of resilience. That planning is a form of generosity, and managing money wisely isn't a distraction because **it's what protects the mission.**

This is the turning point. When your people and policies align, your strategy becomes more than a document; it becomes a shared identity.

And that's what prepares you for the next step: growth.

Key Takeaways for Your Mission

- **Speak in Mission Language, Not Wall Street Jargon**
  To get buy-in from your staff and board, and to frame financial strategy in terms of impact, sustainability, and stewardship instead of citing theoretical returns and investments. You can avoid losing anyone by focusing on your program instead of "finance-speak."

- **Set Clear Financial Guardrails**
  Simple internal policies such as minimum operating cash, reserve usage rules, and investment policies help reduce fear and build shared confidence in your plan.

- **Unite the Mission-Driven and the Risk-Averse**
  Address the tension between short-term urgency and long-term planning by showing how financial strategy protects the mission and aligns with your organization's values.

- **Open Books > Closed Doors**
  Present your strategy visually, share real-life examples, and make space for open discussion where everyone feels invited to the table. The more people understand the plan, the more likely they are to support it, helping ensure your organization thrives financially.

CHAPTER 8

Growing with Guardrails

When it comes to money, most nonprofits are taught to be cautious. Conservative. Risk-averse. Don't spend too much. Don't save too much. But that doesn't mean to not explore investing.

Here's the truth: **nonprofits can, and should, invest**. Not recklessly. Not aggressively. But wisely, and strategically, so that the dollars you already have can work on behalf of the mission you're building every day.

Investing for a nonprofit doesn't mean day trading in risky stocks or going all-in on tech shares. In fact, that's specifically something you should not do! Investing should mean conservative, highly diversified holdings curated just for organizations like you.

In this chapter, we're going to explore how to take the next step in your nonprofit's financial strategy by building smart investment policies that protect your mission, generate sustainable growth, and help align your board and leadership team. Think of it as building guardrails that free you to move forward with confidence.

Building a strategy for the future means bringing people with you. When your team understands the vision and sees their role in making it happen, that's when real momentum takes hold.

From "We've Never Done This Before" to "We're Doing This Right"

Let's start with the elephant in the boardroom: fear. For many nonprofits, investing feels risky. Unknown. Maybe even off-limits. If you've ever heard someone say, *"We've never done that before,"* you're not alone.

The problem isn't just the lack of reserves many nonprofits face. It's the lack of belief that reserves could be possible and that those reserves could be productive. It's the lack of people and processes to manage the investment of these funds.

The truth? Every major university, hospital, and foundation you've ever heard of invests. Most of them have endowments, and they all have healthy reserve funds that generate income to sustain their missions year after year. This is public data readily available online if you'd like to delve deeper.

This is standard practice for well-run, nationally recognized tax-exempt organizations. Why not you too?

Why Nonprofits Should Invest

Let's look at a hypothetical example. If you're leaving $500,000 in a standard checking or savings account earning 0.01% interest, you're making $50 a year.

Now imagine that same $500,000 in a conservative, diversified reserve portfolio earning a 5% average return. That's potentially up to $25,000 a year in passive income for money that could fund programs, staff, or operational needs without a single donor being asked.

Same funding, but managed differently.

Even better? Growth typically compounds over time. In 10 years, without touching the principal, that $500,000 could become more than $814,000. That's the power of compound interest and thoughtful stewardship.

Start with Mission, Not Markets

When the topic of investing comes up, it's easy for nonprofit leaders to get caught in the weeds of market performance or risk. Investing is about sustaining your mission, not beating the market

Remember: most donor wealth is already invested in the market. When they give to your organization, they're often doing so out of assets that have grown there. If you believe the market is destined to collapse long-term, that same concern would apply to your donor base; their wealth would disappear, too. The very fact that donors give generously is a signal of their trust that markets, over time, grow and create opportunity.

Nonprofits can lean on that same confidence. Investing reserves is not speculation; it's stewardship. You're not simply managing money but you're managing trust, stability, and the future of your mission. The key is to design an investment strategy aligned with your organization's timelines and values, guided by purpose rather than performance alone.

So how do you begin?

Translating Investment Language into Mission Outcomes

The first step is reframing the conversation. Don't ask, *"Should we invest?"* Instead, try asking, *"How can we better steward our resources to fund our mission today, tomorrow, and ten years from now?"*

When you link dollars to outcomes, investing becomes a tool, not a gamble.

For example:

- A reserve fund helps you keep your team employed during a funding gap.

- A moderate growth strategy helps you pay for new program pilots next year.

- An endowment supports scholarships for the next generation.

Always connect the financial strategy to the mission strategy. That's what brings people along.

Establishing Guardrails: Your Investment Policy Statement

Think of your **Investment Policy Statement (IPS)** as your nonprofit's financial seatbelt. It protects your values, provides structure, and keeps everyone on the same page.

A strong IPS outlines:

- Your investment goals

- Risk tolerance

- Liquidity needs

- Spending and withdrawal policies

- Roles and responsibilities

- Guidelines for acceptable investments

An IPS doesn't need to be complicated. It just needs to be clear, thoughtful, and aligned with your mission. It helps ensure your board isn't making reactive decisions every time the market moves. Instead, it provides a long-term framework to guide you and your financial team with confidence.

If you don't have one yet, don't worry. You can build it together with your advisor and your board. We have an IPS template in the Appendix of this book to get you going!

Just remember to start small and revise your IPS as you grow.

Understanding Risk Tolerance for Nonprofits

Risk is a loaded word. But in nonprofit investing, risk doesn't mean recklessness; it means being honest about the tradeoffs between growth, liquidity, and stability. We can never avoid risk entirely, but we can manage it intentionally.

Start by asking the right questions:

- **What's our mission time horizon?** Are we planning for one year or twenty? The longer your time horizon, the more room you have to ride out market fluctuations and earn stronger returns.

- **What are our liquidity needs?** Will we need access to this money next month, or can it stay invested for the next year, or even for five years?

- **How diverse and reliable is our funding base?** Do we have multiple revenue sources, or are we dependent on a few major funders?

- **How do our board and leadership emotionally respond to volatility?** Can they weather a temporary dip without overreacting, or do they need more peace of mind?

If you need the funds in the next few months, safety and accessibility should be your top priorities, but that doesn't mean leaving it in your checking account. That means parking short-term cash in insured accounts, money market funds, or short-term Treasuries.

For money you don't need for at least a year, such as operational reserves, capital reserves, or future program investments, you can begin considering mid to longer-term strategies.

This is where **low-risk, highly liquid investment options** such as laddered bond portfolios or diversified fixed income strategies come into play. These allow your funds to grow conservatively, while still remaining accessible when needed. As your reserve levels grow, you can segment funds based on their intended purpose and timeline, thus creating different "buckets" of capital aligned with your financial needs.

No matter your strategy, **diversification is essential**. A well-diversified portfolio spreads funds across different asset classes (like bonds, cash equivalents, and equities) so that one market event doesn't jeopardize your entire reserve. Over time, it can be one of the most effective tools for reducing risk and creating reliable, steady growth over longer time horizons.

Bottom line? Align your investments with your responsibilities. Know what money is for today, what's for tomorrow, and what's for the future, and allocate each accordingly. That's stewardship, and it's one of the smartest financial decisions your nonprofit can make.

Taking the First Steps Towards Sustainability

If your nonprofit doesn't have a reserve fund, don't panic. But don't wait either. We all start at zero. Here's what you can do now:

- **Understand your monthly cash needs** – What's sitting idle in a checking or savings account today? Anything not needed in the next six months may be a candidate for a reserve fund. To estimate your monthly needs, take your total spend over the last year and divide by 12. For more on this, please check out our Operating Expense Calculator Worksheet in the Appendix.

- **Set a goal** – Best practice recommends building reserves equal to six to 12 months of operating expenses. Your actual number may vary based on your funding diversity and cash flow consistency. Once you've established your desired threshold, additional funds can be used to seed endowments, start new programs, or take on longer-term growth and planning.

- **Start small** – Allocate 5-10% of unrestricted gifts to a reserve fund. If you're running a capital campaign, consider adding 10% to cover operating reserves.

- **Build a policy** – Work with your board to define how reserves will be used and invested in accordance with your IPS template. Examples to include are:

    o "The Board will review this Investment Policy Statement annually."

    o "Operational Reserves should be maintained in a separate account and maintained with at least six months of operational expenses."

    o "The withdrawal of Reserve Funds will be determined when needs arise outside of traditional and/or expected operating expenses."

- **Steward wisely** – Avoid parking large sums in low-yield accounts. Choose conservative, highly liquid investments that are designed to be accessible but still earn reasonable growth.

- **Report transparently** – Tell your board, your staff, and even your donors why you're saving. Show them how your reserve strategy protects your mission.

The Gift That Could Have Been More

A small charter school receives a one-time, unrestricted gift of $250,000. The leadership is overjoyed. Unsure of what the future holds, they tuck it away in a bank account "just in case."

Three years pass. They dip into it here and there, covering a gap in the budget, funding a small project, without a clear policy or plan. Meanwhile, inflation quietly eats away at its buying power. When they finally check the balance, it's down to $112,000, and worth even less in real terms.

Now imagine a different outcome with the same gift but there is a simple Investment Policy Statement in place. The funds are placed in a diversified reserve strategy earning 5% annually, with withdrawals only for board-approved initiatives.

Three years later, instead of shrinking, the gift has grown to over $289,000, **while still supporting real, mission-aligned projects along the way.**

Stewardship is about multiplying your gifts with wisdom and purpose, so every donor dollar goes further, every year.

The difference between the first story and the second isn't luck. It's leadership. And your mission deserves the second story.

Choosing the Right Fiduciary Partners

Now that you know the *why* and the *how*, let's talk about the *who*.

Managing nonprofit investments requires the right kind of support. This is not a job for your banker, your cousin, or a friend who "knows the stock market." Not even for a seasoned, well-intentioned board member (and the good ones typically will tell you that).

You need a true **fiduciary partner**, a licensed, unbiased, professional, and registered financial advisor who is legally bound to act in your organization's best interest. Specifically, you need more than a volunteer or board member with an inherent understanding of nonprofit investment strategies.

Here's what to look for in your nonprofit's financial advisor:

- Fiduciary responsibility (not a broker, banker, or product salesperson)

- Nonprofit-specific experience

- The ability to write or review your Investment Policy Statement

- Conservative, mission-aligned strategies

- Transparent and affordable fees

- Clear, accessible reporting

- Ease of communication and education

Nonprofit leaders are busy. The right advisor should simplify your life, not complicate it. They should make board reporting easier, not more intimidating. They should be a thought partner to come alongside you, not just another vendor.

Why Traditional Wealth Managers Often Miss the Mark

Traditional wealth managers and private banks are typically built around personal or corporate wealth and not institutional stewardship. Their advice often centers on maximizing returns instead of the unique needs of nonprofits, such as liquidity planning, governance oversight, donor intent, board reporting, and policy creation.

Nonprofits require a different lens. One that balances growth, mission, and risk and understands the extra layers of complexity that come with being tax-exempt, donor-funded, and impact-driven.

That's why we started Infinite Giving. We're nonprofit leaders too, and we saw firsthand how few financial partners truly understood this space. Our approach is simple: help organizations set the right goals, craft clear policies, and grow with purpose, not pressure. We believe in full transparency, practical guidance, and ongoing support.

Whether you work with us or someone else, the most important thing is to choose a partner who gets it. One who speaks the language of nonprofits, not just finance, and who shows up with both expertise and empathy.

Avoiding Common Pitfalls

As you begin, or refine, your investment journey, here are the most common mistakes we see:

✗ Keeping funds in a bank
Banks are great for operating cash, but reserves and endowments can often find a better home.

✗ Chasing high returns
Trying to "beat the market" can backfire. Stay mission-focused and risk-aware.

✗ Overconcentration
Putting all your funds in one type of asset or strategy increases vulnerability.

✗ No policy enforcement
Having an IPS is great. Following it is better. Review your IPS regularly with your board and then adjust when needed.

✗ Lack of oversight
Don't DIY. And, even if you're working with a professional, third-party Advisor, your board still needs to understand and oversee strategy. You are better together.

✗ No transparency
Your board and leadership should have access to reporting and know how funds are performing.

From Surviving to Sustaining

Investing is about planning wisely, stewarding responsibly, and positioning your mission to thrive. It means you're building strength.

Conservative, well-structured financial strategies, guided by clear policies and trusted advisors, allow your resources to grow without compromising your values or stability. That growth fuels opportunity. It creates breathing room, resilience, and the ability to say "yes" to more impact.

Start with intention. Because remember, this is about funding your mission, and your mission deserves a future that's not only sustainable, but abundant.

Next Steps for Your Team

- Review your current cash accounts. Are you holding more than you need in checking?

- Audit your current holdings. What are the current yield rates?

- Schedule a board discussion around reserve goals and policies.

- If you don't have an IPS, make it your next board action item.

- Interview potential fiduciary partners.

- Consider nonprofit expertise, fees, and specialized services.

- Celebrate small wins.

Reserve Strategy Matrix: Matching Money to Mission Timing

Reserve Type	Time Horizon	Purpose	Risk Tolerance	Recommended Strategy	Sample Investment Vehicles
Operational Reserves	6-12 months	Cover ongoing payroll, rent, programs, and emergencies	Low	Prioritize liquidity and capital preservation	High-yield savings, money market, short-term Treasuries, fixed income
Capital Reserves	12-18 months	Maintenance and repairs for assets	Low to Moderate	Preserve value with some growth opportunity	Laddered CDARs, ultra-short bond funds, conservative fixed income portfolios
Project and Campaign funds	1 – 3 years	Fund pilot programs, investments in growth	Low to Moderate	Balance liquidity with moderate returns	Diversified fixed income, short-duration bond portfolios
Longer-term Reserves	3 – 5 years	Fund facilities, technology, or long-term projects	Moderate	Focus on long-term preservation and conservative growth	Diversified portfolios with some equity allocation
Endowment Funds	5-10+ years	Provide ongoing annual support for programs	Long-term growth	Maximize sustainable growth with annual spending policies	Fully diversified portfolios aligned with IPS guidelines

CHAPTER 9

Endowments – The Ultimate Long-Term Financial Sustainability

At a board meeting one fall, a long-serving executive director named Monica shared exciting news: a donor had pledged a six-figure gift. But with one condition: it needed to be put toward an endowment. The board chair leaned forward and asked, "Isn't an endowment just for universities and hospitals? Do small nonprofits even do that?"

The room went quiet. Monica didn't have an answer. Yet.

That question "*Are we ready for an endowment?*" is one many nonprofit leaders wrestle with. Endowments can feel distant or daunting, reserved for legacy institutions with deep pockets. But the truth is, you don't need to be big to think long-term. You just need to be strategic.

Unfortunately, many nonprofits never even get the chance to wrestle with the question.

A few years ago, a regional arts organization received a call from a longtime supporter. The donor was finalizing their estate and wanted to leave a meaningful gift: an endowment that would support the organization for decades to come. But the board wasn't ready. They hesitated, asked to reduce the restrictions, and delayed making a decision. So, the donor gave the gift elsewhere.

That story isn't unique. Organizations of all sizes miss out on transformational gifts every year, and not because donors aren't generous but because the organization simply isn't prepared. They haven't built up a strong financial foundation or drafted policies. They haven't created the structure to say yes when the moment comes. Some haven't even had the conversation.

Let's change that.

In this chapter, we'll demystify endowments, explore whether they're right for your organization, and offer practical guidance to build one, step by step. Because while endowments aren't the first step toward financial sustainability, they are often the strongest next one.

And the best time to prepare is before the big gift arrives.

What Is a Nonprofit Endowment?

An endowment is a pool of funds, either donor-restricted or board-designated, invested for the long term to preserve and grow the principal while generating ongoing income for the organization.

Instead of spending the entire gift, the nonprofit distributes only a small percentage each year, typically around 4–5%, based on a rolling multi-year average from the investment returns. This steady distribution supports the mission while the principal remains intact, continuing to earn for years to come.

Unlike reserve funds, which are meant for short- to medium-term needs such as emergencies or planned projects, an endowment is built to last. It's a perpetual gift, a well that never runs dry, designed to fund your mission not just today, but for generations.

This is what makes endowments unique: they're not quick wins, but slow, steady, strategic investments in your future. They require patience, clear policies, and diligent oversight. And in return, they offer something every nonprofit needs: **predictable funding.**

This gives your organization the margin to:

- Weather economic downturns

- Grow thoughtfully

- Plan with confidence instead of reacting in a crisis

An endowment is a single gift that can provide for your mission year after year, decade after decade. It's one of the most powerful tools for long-term sustainability a nonprofit can build.

Not Just for Ivy League Institutions

When many people hear the word "endowment," they picture billion-dollar university funds or legacy healthcare systems with named buildings and elite financial teams. And it's true – large institutions have long used endowments to fuel their growth, fund scholarships, and secure their futures, because they work.

Despite their size today, it's important to remember that they all started at nothing. But with strategy, patience, and time, those funds have grown to be incredibly impactful.

The good news is that endowments are no longer reserved just for the few, and they are no longer off-limits to smaller tax-exempt organizations.

In fact, **smaller and mid-sized organizations may need them even more**. When your budget relies on unpredictable grants or seasonal fundraising cycles, a steady stream of endowment income, even modest, can stabilize your planning and reduce dependence on short-term funding wins.

That said, endowments at smaller organizations tend to look a bit different. They're more likely to take the form of **quasi-**

endowments, initiated by the board using unrestricted reserves or major gifts. They often start smaller, for example $250,000, and are invested conservatively. Often there's less appetite for high volatility – and that's okay.

An experienced nonprofit Advisor will understand that smaller endowments are typically managed differently than billion-dollar ones. Governance may also be more informal at first, guided by policies rather than large committees.

But the fundamentals remain the same. The goal is to preserve the principal, generate income, and align the fund with the organization's mission, values, and needs.

What matters is not how big your endowment is. What matters is whether you've thought intentionally about how you'd build one, manage it, and communicate its purpose when the opportunity arises.

Why Build an Endowment?

There's something profound about planting a tree whose shade you may never sit under. That's what endowments are. They're an act of faith, and a commitment to the mission beyond the current fiscal year.

But they're also practical.

A well-structured endowment creates **predictable, unrestricted income** that can support staff positions, program expansion, innovation, or basic operations. That steady stream, even if small, reduces the pressure on annual fundraising and enables better financial planning.

Endowments also attract donors. Especially high-net-worth individuals and legacy givers. Why? Because endowments represent permanence. Donors know their gift won't be spent all at once. It will be invested, honored, and extended far into the future. That's appealing. It turns a one-time donation into a sustainable legacy.

For generous donors, particularly, this is deeply meaningful. For nonprofits, it can be deeply stabilizing.

6 Types of Endowment Funds

Not all endowments look alike, and that's a good thing. One of the biggest misconceptions nonprofit leaders face is that endowments must be large, permanent, and heavily restricted. In reality, endowments come in many shapes and sizes, each offering different levels of flexibility, donor involvement, and strategic fit.

Understanding these types will help you identify what kind of endowment could work best for your organization today and how you might evolve it over time.

1. True Endowment

Also known as a **permanent endowment**, this can be a donor-restricted or unrestricted gift and one where the principal must be held in perpetuity. Only the earnings can be spent, typically following a set disbursement policy (such as 4–5% annually). These endowments often align closely with the donor's long-term vision and are legally binding. They are common in higher education and healthcare institutions. Think of the Ford Family Foundation or the Rockefeller Foundation.

2. Restricted Endowment

In a restricted endowment, the **purpose** of the earnings, not just the permanence, is designated by the donor. For example, a donor may fund an endowment to support a specific program, scholarship, position, or department. These endowments offer predictable funding for targeted needs but may create rigidity over time. Nonprofits should enter into restricted agreements carefully, ensuring the restriction aligns with the long-term mission.

3. Unrestricted Endowment

One of the **most desirable types** of endowment for a nonprofit. In this structure, the endowment is either board-designated or donor-gifted with the freedom to use the annual earnings wherever they're needed most. While the principal is still preserved, the flexibility of the disbursement allows organizations to respond to evolving needs and opportunities. If you can shape donor conversations to support unrestricted endowment giving, your organization's sustainability options grow significantly.

4. Term Endowment

A term endowment is similar to a true endowment, with one key difference: it has a **built-in expiration date**. The principal may be spent after a specific period of time (such as 10 or 20 years), or when certain conditions are met. This structure offers a middle ground between long-term growth and eventual access to the full gift. Term endowments can be especially appealing to donors who want to see both immediate and lasting impact.

5. Quasi-Endowment

Another popular option is a **board-designated endowment**, also known as a quasi-endowment that is created by the nonprofit itself using unrestricted funds typically from reserves, surplus gifts, or one-time windfalls. It functions just like an endowment, but the board retains the authority to access the principal if necessary. This makes it an ideal structure for smaller or mid-sized organizations that want to start building long-term funds without permanent restrictions. Quasi-endowments are often the *first step* into endowment territory for nonprofits learning how to think in decades, not just years.

6. Micro-Endowment

A micro-endowment is a **small-scale endowment**, often seeded with $25,000 – $50,000, designed to make long-term giving accessible to a wider range of donors. These funds can grow significantly over time and still follow the standard investment and disbursement practices. Micro-endowments are especially useful for engaging mid-level or legacy donors who want to create something lasting, even if they don't have millions to give. When promoted well, a network of micro-endowments can have collective power and long-term impact.

Each of these structures has its place in a healthy nonprofit ecosystem. The best endowment for your organization is the one that fits your current readiness, donor interest, and strategic goals.

It's important to remember modern financial tools make setting up and maintaining these possible – something that would have been too expensive and time-consuming with legacy banking. Plus, your organization has benefitted by creating mission-aligned endowments before the donor approaches with a major gift.

And never forget: **you don't need to start big. You just need to thoughtfully start.**

Overcoming the Barriers to Building an Endowment

With all that said, endowments are not a silver bullet and not for every organization. They require a solid foundation and a long view.

While most funders view an endowment as a sign of financial sustainability, there are a few who see it differently (which blows my mind). Every now and then, you may run into a grantmaker who hesitates to give if you already have an endowment, assuming it means you don't "need" their support. This mindset can feel counterintuitive.

The good news is that this barrier can usually be overcome by being transparent and showing how your endowment is built for long-term stability while today's donations still fuel immediate impact. When funders see that both are true, most are reassured and remain engaged.

That said, external perceptions aren't the only hurdles. Some of the biggest barriers come from within your own organization, specifically whether you have the right financial foundation in place. Before you launch one, you need both the right resources and the right mindset.

The first and most practical barrier is not having healthy reserves. If your organization doesn't already have at least six to 12 months of operating reserves, an endowment is premature. Reserves give you the flexibility to make payroll next month or respond to an urgent community need. Endowments, by contrast, are built for the next decade and beyond. They're not cash flow tools; they're continuity tools. Your organization must establish short-term sustainability before moving into long-term planning.

Another common barrier is mindset. Scarcity culture keeps leaders focused on today's crises and blinds them to tomorrow's opportunities. When you're used to scraping by, it can feel almost irresponsible to save for the future. But that's often the exact moment when it's most important to start. Even a modest endowment, funded by a single donor gift or a small internal transfer, can shift your culture. It sends a message to your board, donors, and community: "We plan to be here tomorrow."

Board hesitation can also slow progress. If your board is unfamiliar with investment policies, uneasy about restricted gifts, or simply resistant to new approaches, the concept of an endowment may feel like uncharted territory. Education is the antidote here. Share examples of similar organizations that have used endowments to multiply their mission.

Finally, there's the fear of complexity. What policies do we need? How should we invest? Who will manage it? These are valid questions, and they have answers. With the right advisor, you'll have guidance on every step: from setting policies and structuring governance to aligning investments with your mission and donor intent.

The barriers are real, but they're not permanent. With preparation, education, and partnership, you can begin building an endowment that supports your mission for generations to come.

Big Gifts Go Where There's Infrastructure

Let's talk candidly about major donors.

Generous donors want to give in deeply meaningful ways: gifts that reflect their values, their legacy, and their love for your mission. But when it comes to large or planned gifts, they don't just want to give meaningfully but they also want to give wisely. They want to know their generosity will last.

That's why endowments are so attractive to many of these donors. Endowments feel permanent. They say, "This gift will outlive me. It will support the cause I care about long after I'm gone." That kind of emotional resonance is powerful. For many donors, it's the most satisfying form of giving in a single act of generosity that continues bearing fruit for generations.

But here's the challenge: big gifts tend to go to the institutions that are ready to receive them.

Why? Because they have the infrastructure and make it easy for donors. Large organizations (universities, hospitals, and national nonprofits) often have dedicated gift officers, clear policies, established endowment accounts, and outside fiduciary advisors. They also have the marketing plans and programs to ask for those big gifts and are built to steward them well. And donors notice.

Smaller and mid-sized nonprofits, on the other hand, often miss out. And it's not because they lack the mission or the donor relationships, but because they haven't put the right systems in place. Without a reserve fund, a fiduciary partner, or a clear endowment policy, these organizations unintentionally send a message: *We're not quite ready.*

Think about it this way: when a donor does give a significant gift to an unprepared organization, what often happens? The money gets spent down within a few years. There's no strategy to protect or grow it. No disbursement plan. No legacy. Just a brief burst of abundance, followed by a return to scarcity. That doesn't inspire donor confidence. And so, the next big gift goes elsewhere.

This creates a familiar cycle: large institutions grow wealthier, while smaller nonprofits struggle to build capital. But that cycle can be broken.

Start by building healthy reserves. Draft simple endowment policies. Open an account. Seed it, even with a smaller amount, and practice telling the story. "This is our endowment. It's here to support our mission not just this year, but forever." That kind of language signals maturity, vision, and readiness.

So, when the right donor comes along, and they will, you won't be scrambling. You'll be ready. Not just to accept the gift, but to honor it for decades to come.

And you'll be able to say, with full confidence, "Yes. We're ready to carry this forward."

How to Build an Endowment from Scratch

If you're ready to begin, start by building alignment. Talk with your board about the purpose of an endowment. Emphasize that this is about permanence and the continuity of your important work, not liquidity. You're thinking about how to leave a financial legacy, not just funding next year's budget.

Then move into structure. The easiest place to start is with a **quasi-endowment** that is a board-designated fund using unrestricted reserves or a major gift. Because it's not donor-restricted, the board retains flexibility while still signaling long-term thinking. This can be a powerful stepping stone to future true endowments.

You'll also need a few core documents:

- An **Investment Policy Statement (IPS)** that defines how the endowment can be invested, disbursed, and managed.

- An **Endowment Agreement** is often an addendum to the IPS and typically outlines the structure and purpose of the fund.

- A **Usage Policy** that clarifies how income may or may not be used, and whether any restrictions apply

  Note – sometimes an IPS and/or Endowment Policy includes this.

With those pieces in place, choose an investment partner who understands nonprofits. Avoid retail advisors or banks unfamiliar with endowment structures. You need a fiduciary with nonprofit-specific expertise, a financial advisor who can help you build policies, communicate with donors, and manage disbursements with transparency and care.

Once the account is open, begin funding it. This might come from a single donor, a percentage of campaign revenue, or a designated portion of annual unrestricted gifts. Even a 5–10% allocation from surplus income can add up over time.

Then, tell the story of legacy. Make endowment giving visible. Honor donors who support it. And let your community know: **this gift and our work will outlive us all.**

Case Study: A Legacy That Grew

Ten years ago, a domestic violence shelter in the Southeast received a modest bequest of $75,000. Their board wasn't sure what to do with it. Spend it on program expansion? Put it into reserves?

Instead, they did something bold. They created a quasi-endowment to seed a legacy impact.

They partnered with a nonprofit investment advisor who helped them draft a simple IPS and disbursement policy. They invested the funds conservatively, aiming for a 4–5% annual distribution. The first year's earnings were just over $3,000 but they used it to fund emergency hotel stays for survivors. That small act made the endowment feel real.

Over time, other donors began to notice. When the organization launched a legacy campaign a few years later, they had something concrete to offer: a permanent endowment that would support women and families for decades to come. This opened the pathway for more major legacy gifts.

Today, their endowment has grown to more than $1,000,000 and consistently funds an annual staff position.

As their executive director said, "It started small. But it made us think bigger and longer term. And now, it's part of our giving culture and a cornerstone of our financial planning."

3 Signs You're Ready for an Endowment

Not every organization is ready for an endowment today... but many are closer than they think. Here's how you know it might be time:

1. You Have Healthy Reserves

Your organization already has six to 12 months of operating reserves set aside and isn't in crisis mode. You've moved beyond survival and have a strong foundation in place.

2. Your Board Thinks Long-Term

Your board is aligned around strategic planning and financial sustainability. They're willing to adopt and follow investment and disbursement policies over multiple years.

3. Donors Are Asking About Legacy Giving

You've had donors express interest in estate gifts, restricted gifts, or endowments, or you sense they're ready to give more, if you had the right structure in place.

*If you can say "yes" to two or more of these, your organization may be more ready than you think to finally start an endowment.

Final Thoughts: Thinking in Decades

Endowments aren't a starting point because they aren't for everyone. However, endowments are a key milestone in the health and sustainability of many nonprofit organizations, and one we wish more organizations considered. Donors give legacy gifts, but the question is, are you open to them?

You don't have to start with millions. You can start with a single donor. You can start with a portion of your reserves. You can start with a single policy or a board vote to think not just about this fiscal year, but the next generation.

And when you do, you'll find yourself building more than a financial fund. You'll be building confidence, trust, and long-term mission alignment that will serve your community for decades to come and open up new pathways for major gifts.

Because the organizations that thrive tomorrow are the ones who *plan* for tomorrow, starting today.

Key Takeaways for Your Mission

- **Endowments Are About Permanence, Not Cash Flow**

  They're designed to preserve and grow principal while generating steady income year after year, funding your mission for decades, not next month's payroll.

- **Small and Mid-Sized Nonprofits Can (and Should) Build Them**

  You don't need millions to start. Even a modest quasi-endowment can shift your culture toward long-term thinking and signal stability to donors.

- **Utilize Technology and Financial Partners**

  By leveraging modern financial tools and professional management, you can start small and be well-positioned to receive significant long-term gifts.

- **Healthy Reserves Come First**

  Before launching an endowment, ensure you have at least six to 12 months of operating reserves to handle emergencies and maintain operational flexibility.

- **Readiness Attracts Major Gifts**

  Donors are more likely to fund an endowment when they see you have the policies, accounts, and investment partners in place to steward their gift wisely.

- **Start Now, Grow Over Time**

  Seed your endowment with a portion of reserves, a single donor gift, or campaign revenue. Tell the story about building legacy early so donors know they can help grow it.

CHAPTER 10

Unlocking Stock, Crypto, and Donor-Advised Fund Giving

Most nonprofit leaders are focused on one thing when it comes to fundraising: bringing in more cash.

Annual campaigns, event sponsorships, and year-end appeals are the tools we know. They feel tangible, familiar, and immediate. But in the effort to secure more annual gifts, many organizations overlook the single most transformative source of support available to them: **non-cash giving.**

We're not just talking about writing bigger checks. We're talking about gifts of stock, cryptocurrency, donor-advised fund (DAF) grants, and even complex assets such as real estate and private equity. These types of gifts make up the majority of donor wealth yet remain the least accessed by many nonprofits.

Why?

Because non-cash giving has a reputation: it feels complicated, confusing, even intimidating. Many nonprofit leaders assume their donors aren't asking to give in these ways, or that their organization isn't big enough to be considered. But that's not the real problem. The real issue is **readiness.**

Major donors are already giving these kinds of gifts. If you aren't receiving them, it simply means they're giving them to someone else and most likely to the prepared organizations that make it easy.

Non-cash giving isn't just a nice-to-have; it's the key to unlocking a new level of generosity. And if your organization wants to grow sustainably, you can't afford to ignore it.

This chapter will show you how to shift your mindset, put the right infrastructure in place, and confidently ask for and receive the kinds of gifts that build long-term capacity. Because once you're ready, those gifts will come. And they can change everything.

The Hidden Gem of Stock Giving

A few years ago, a mid-sized environmental nonprofit in the Pacific Northwest received an email from a longtime donor.

The donor, who had supported the organization with $1,000 gifts for several years, was planning to make a more significant contribution. However, instead of writing a check, he wanted to donate $100,000 in appreciated stock.

The problem? The organization didn't have a brokerage account. No one on staff knew how to accept a stock donation, and the board was hesitant to invest the time and effort to set up a new system. "We've never done this before," someone said. "This feels complex. What if we do all of this work and then never get another stock donation?"

After weeks of delay, the donor got tired of waiting. They needed the tax efficiencies this type of gift could bring them so instead they donated it to another nonprofit doing similar work.

That gift, which could have funded a year's worth of programming or created a quasi-endowment, was gone. Not because the donor wasn't generous, but because the infrastructure wasn't in place.

Two years later, the nonprofit became proactive. They opened a brokerage account, established a basic stock gift policy, plus trained staff on how to talk about the tax efficiencies of this type of giving and walk a donor through the process.

That same year, another donor, this time a foundation trustee, asked if they could make a gift from their family's holdings. This time, the answer was easy and confident: "Absolutely."

That single gift led to a new relationship and $250,000 in multi-year funding.

The difference? **Readiness.**

This nonprofit didn't launch a capital campaign. They didn't hire a new development officer. They didn't send out elaborate direct mail appeals. They just opened the door, and generosity walked through.

That's the real power of asset giving. It's not just about dollars; think of it as unleashing new generosity by removing barriers.

Why Asset Gifts Matter More Than Ever

Let's look at the data.

According to Dr. Russell James' groundbreaking study, *Cash is Not King*, nonprofits that consistently raised gifts from assets such as stocks, real estate, or business interests saw fundraising growth rates **six times greater** over five years than organizations accepting only cash gifts. For mid-sized nonprofits, those raising between $100,000 and $1 million annually, the results were even more dramatic: seven times more fundraising growth when gifts of securities were part of the mix.

This wasn't a fluke or limited to one sector. The trend held across all 26 major nonprofit cause categories, from education to environmental work, from healthcare to human services.

In every case, organizations that can receive gifts of appreciated assets outperformed their cash-only counterparts. Why? Because they were tapping into where real wealth lives.

Here's the key insight: according to the U.S. Census Bureau's Survey of Income and Program Participation (SIPP), **over 90% of household wealth in America is held in non-cash assets** such as stocks, real estate, and business equity. Only a small fraction of a donor's financial life lives in their checking account. So, when we only ask for cash, we're asking from their smallest bucket of wealth. It's no wonder that limits the size and scope of the gifts we receive.

Gifts of stock also offer donors powerful tax advantages. By donating appreciated stocks, they can avoid up to 37% in capital gains taxes and receive a deduction for the full fair market value of the gift. For many donors, stock giving is the most cost-effective and generous way to support the causes they care about.

Even crypto, still a fairly emerging giving vehicle, has demonstrated staying power. According to The Giving Block, in 2021, over $300 million in cryptocurrency was donated to U.S. nonprofits. The organizations with the infrastructure in place to receive crypto gifts saw tremendous upside.

This isn't theory. This is real, measurable, donor-backed momentum.

If your nonprofit isn't prepared to accept these asset gifts, then you're missing out on significant donations. Plus, you're cutting yourself off from the highest-capacity, most tax-savvy, legacy-minded donors in your community.

The Chicken and the Egg Problem in Nonprofit Giving

Still, many nonprofits hesitate.

They say, "We've never received a stock gift before," or "Our donors haven't asked us about cryptocurrency," and take that as a signal that there's no need to prepare. But this thinking is a trap, and it creates a loop of perpetual missed opportunity.

It's also understandable. Nonprofit leaders and boards are often overloaded. They want to focus on what's most urgent, most tangible, most immediate. So, when a donor hasn't explicitly asked to give stock, crypto, or a DAF grant, those options fall to the bottom of the list, or off the radar entirely.

But here's the truth: **donors rarely ask first, nor do foundations.**

Sophisticated donors and grant makers, the kind who are giving appreciated assets, are thinking about tax advantages and/or making estate plans, assuming that the organizations they give to are ready. However, if you don't mention stock giving on your website, if you can't clearly explain how to give from a DAF, if you don't have a brokerage account or a strategy for accepting non-cash gifts, **they often won't ask.** Instead, they'll simply give to the organization that *is* ready.

And so, the cycle continues.

Your team waits for a donor to express interest. The donor waits for a sign that you can handle the gift. Neither makes a move. And in the end, that transformational donation goes to a university, hospital, or national charity that already has the infrastructure and language in place to invite the donor into the most tax-efficient vehicle of giving.

This is what we call the 'Chicken and the Egg Problem' of non-cash giving.

But here's the good news: **you can break the cycle.**

You don't need to wait for a donor to ask before getting prepared. In fact, you shouldn't. Being ready before the ask is what sets successful, sustainable organizations apart. Building a non-cash giving strategy is not only about logistics, but it's also about signaling to your donors that you're thinking bigger, planning long-term, and capable of stewarding meaningful generosity.

You might not have received a stock gift yet, but that doesn't mean one isn't coming. Don't wait until opportunity knocks to build the door.

Why Stocks and Cryptocurrency? And Why Now?

Stock and crypto ownership have risen. According to the Federal Reserve Board's Survey of Consumer Finances, stock ownership among U.S. households has grown significantly over the past few decades. In 1989, only about 32% of households owned stocks.

The most recent data shows that by 2022, **58% of U.S. households held stocks**, either directly or indirectly through mutual funds, retirement accounts, or other vehicles (SEC, 2024). And this number continues to rise.

For nonprofits, this trend represents a major opportunity. As more families hold wealth in the markets rather than in cash, the potential for non-cash giving (particularly stock donations) continues to grow.

Some of your donors are likely also getting into the **$3 trillion+** crypto market. Virtually worthless a decade ago, the value of a single Bitcoin reached its **all-time high of $122,979** in July 2025, according to Coinbase.

Asset-based giving is no longer a trend. It's the future of generosity, and it's already here. Research from Dr. Russell James published on EncourageGenerosity.com shows that over the past decade, **gifts of appreciated securities to**

nonprofits have surged by 136%. What used to be considered "advanced" philanthropy is quickly becoming standard practice for informed donors.

By preparing to receive gifts of stock and crypto, nonprofits can invite generosity from a much larger pool of wealth. The average online cash gift may be modest, but asset gifts are often significantly larger and carry unique tax advantages for donors, making them a win-win for both the donor and the mission.

Thanks to modern financial tools and platforms, ease is also an important part of the equation. The more frictionless you can make the process, the better. Generous givers should be able to initiate stock or crypto gifts quickly and securely. Technology now makes this once painful process seamless on both the donor and administrative sides.

Let's break it down with an example.

As mentioned, when a donor gives appreciated stock or crypto assets directly to a nonprofit, they can avoid paying up to 37% in capital gains taxes while still receiving a charitable deduction for the full fair market value of the asset. That means a donor contributing $100,000 in stock might save $30,000 or more in taxes compared to simply giving cash.

And yes, the IRS currently treats crypto gifts the same as stocks in this regard. That means Bitcoin, Ethereum, and other long-term held cryptocurrencies are currently eligible for the same powerful double-benefit: no capital gains tax and a full-value deduction.

Yes, crypto has more volatility. Yes, it comes with some operational nuance. But nonprofits receiving crypto gifts, especially during bull markets, have seen dramatic windfalls. The key is to liquidate quickly and not try to hold or speculate.

For the growing population of individuals who hold both securities and crypto (especially younger, tech-savvy donors), this is a compelling incentive to give generously, but only if nonprofits make it easy to do so.

And yet, many nonprofits don't.

Whether due to outdated systems, limited awareness, or hesitation from boards, nonprofits often restrict the very forms of giving that could unlock larger, more strategic generosity. **However, what we need to remember is that generosity is personal.**

When a donor chooses to give through stock or crypto, they're not just moving money but they're aligning their values with financial stewardship and tax wisdom.

If you're ready to grow beyond the limitations of annual cash campaigns, start by **making it easy for your donors to be generous on their terms.**

How to Receive Stock and Crypto Gifts

Let's break down what this actually looks like in practice.

- **Open a Brokerage Account and Crypto Wallet.** This is your first step. Historically, it's taken weeks or even months to open these types of accounts with plenty of paperwork, minimums, compliance delays, and service fees. Modern partners like Infinite Giving can open them both in just a few business days.

- **Liquidate Automatically.** Best practice is to sell gifts of stock and crypto immediately upon receipt. This prevents market fluctuations from impacting the gift's value and avoids the risk of holding assets that fall out of alignment with your mission or policies.

- **Make It Donor-Friendly.** Include a "Give Stock" and "Give Crypto" button on your donation page and automate what you can. Please don't ask the donor to download a PDF, fill it out, and then still call or email your office. The easier and more visible you make it, the more likely donors are to act.

- **Educate Your Donors.** Many people don't realize how beneficial and tax-efficient asset giving can be. Stock, crypto, DAF, and even endowment giving should be a consistent part of your giving culture and regularly mentioned in asks. Use your newsletters, events, and one-on-one conversations to teach donors about the tax advantages and impact. They'll thank you for it.

DAFs: Great for Donors, Tricky for Nonprofits

Donor-advised funds (DAFs) are one of the fastest-growing vehicles in philanthropy. According to the National Philanthropic Trust, as of 2023, DAFs held more than $250 billion in charitable assets and distributed over $50 billion in grants to nonprofits in that same year.

An interesting note: these numbers continue to climb even amid economic headwinds as donors lean into the flexibility, privacy, and tax advantages of donor-advised funds.

For donors, DAFs are attractive because they combine immediate tax benefits with long-term control over giving decisions. A donor contributes to a DAF, takes an instant tax deduction, and then recommends grants to charities over time. Since DAF balances can be invested, they may even grow, creating more charitable dollars to deploy in the future.

But here's the reality for nonprofits: DAFs weren't designed to serve you; they were designed to serve donors.

Once funds are contributed, they no longer legally belong to the donor but to the sponsoring organization (Fidelity, Schwab, Vanguard, community foundations, or large charities). Donors may recommend grants, but the sponsor has final say, and strict IRS rules apply, such as prohibitions on funding personal benefits like gala tickets, fundraising dinners, auction items, or any gift that provides the donor with a personal benefit (NPT, 2024).

It's also important to know that, unlike private foundations, which must distribute at least 5% of their assets annually, DAFs have no payout requirement. That means funds can sit untouched indefinitely. And unless donors name successor advisors or designate charitable beneficiaries in their wills specifically from their DAF, the remaining balance may be absorbed by the sponsoring organization when the donor passes away and leaves nonprofits with nothing.

So yes, there are challenges. But there's also a great opportunity.

What This Means for Nonprofits

1. **Don't set up your own DAF.** Opening one for your organization means giving up control of your own dollars and often paying high management fees. Instead, focus on positioning your nonprofit to *receive* DAF grants.

2. **Make your nonprofit easy to find.** As of this writing, more than 80% of DAF assets are held by Fidelity Charitable, Schwab Charitable, and National Philanthropic Trust. Make sure your organization is registered and verified with these providers (many use Guidestar/PayPal Giving Fund integration) so donors can seamlessly recommend you for grants.

3. **See DAF donors as top prospects**. Ask for these types of gifts! If a donor has a DAF, it means they already have charitable dollars set aside, funds that must eventually go to nonprofits. This makes them some of your best giving prospects. Engage them thoughtfully, thank them well, and show them why your mission is worthy of their long-term support.

4. **Encourage direct giving where possible.** Donors receive the same tax benefits whether they contribute directly to your nonprofit or into a DAF first. Make it easy for them to give stock, crypto, or other appreciated assets on your website. Direct gifts move dollars to your mission much faster.

The Takeaway

Yes, it can feel frustrating that billions of charitable dollars sit in DAFs instead of flowing directly into nonprofit communities. But the solution isn't to push back against DAFs; it's to make it as easy as possible for donors to move those funds to you.

That means being visible to the largest sponsors, making asset-based giving simple, and stewarding DAF donors with the same care as any major donor. When you show you're ready, willing, and able to receive these grants, you position your nonprofit to capture generosity that might otherwise stay locked up.

Final Thoughts: Let Donors Give from Their Greatest Capacity

When a donor gives from assets, they're giving from their greatest wealth, not just their wallet. These gifts are more than transactions. They're declarations of trust, legacy, and deep alignment with your mission.

And because stocks, crypto, and DAF grants are **the most tax-efficient way for donors to give,** they unlock generosity at a higher level than cash ever could.

Your job is not to pressure donors but to be ready, make the ask, and make it easy. To let them know that whether it's stock, crypto, or a DAF grant, your organization will steward their generosity well.

Because generosity grows where it's welcomed. And donors give more when they know you're ready.

Don't wait for permission. Build the infrastructure, cast the vision, and let donors know the door is open.

The gifts will come.

Did You Know?

Stock and crypto gifts don't include donor names.

When a donor transfers assets, you often won't know who gave unless you have a system in place. Traditional brokerages don't notify you and don't have names attached to transfers, which means missed thank-yous and missed relationships.

Modern tools like Infinite Giving fix that.

They track every donation and automate attribution and liquidation. This makes it easy to thank your donors quickly and personally, so no gift goes unacknowledged, and no donor feels forgotten.

Good stewardship starts with the right systems.

Key Takeaways for Your Mission

- **Non-cash Gifts Unlock Larger Generosity**
  Over 90% of U.S. wealth is held in assets like stocks, real estate, and business equity, not cash. Asking only for cash limits donor capacity.

- **Readiness Drives Results**
  Donors give asset gifts to nonprofits that make it easy. A brokerage account, clear policies, and visible options on your website are essential to attract these gifts.

- **Tax Advantages Make Asset Giving Compelling**
  Stock and crypto donations can save donors up to 37% in capital gains taxes while also giving a deduction for the full fair market value.

- **Break the Chicken and Egg Cycle**
  Don't wait for a donor to ask before preparing. Proactive readiness signals confidence and builds trust with high-capacity, tax-savvy donors.

- **Understand DAFs to Use Them Well**
  Donor-advised funds benefit donors but can delay or reduce nonprofit access to funds. Focus on relationships with DAF donors and encourage those direct gifts.

- **Make it Part of Your Giving Culture**
  Talk about asset giving year-round, train your team, and normalize it in donor conversations so it becomes a natural part of how your community gives. Every ask, every campaign should include multiple giving options that include stock, crypto, and DAF grants, not just credit card transactions.

CHAPTER 11

Preparing for the Great Wealth Transfer

At a recent luncheon, a development director shared a story. A longtime donor, quiet and consistent, had passed away and left their organization a $250,000 surprise bequest. No conversation. No pledge. Just a letter from the estate attorney and a check in the mail.

The team was thrilled. But also a bit stunned.

"We had no idea they were even thinking of us," she said. "What if we had invited that conversation earlier?"

It's a common story, and a powerful one. We're entering a season when these stories will become more frequent, more urgent, and more transformational than anything the nonprofit sector has seen before.

The $124 Trillion Opportunity

Did you know that we are now in the midst of the largest transfer of generational wealth in human history? Over the next two decades, an **estimated $124 trillion in assets** will pass from Baby Boomers to their Gen X, Millennial, and Gen Z heirs, according to the most recent data from Cerulli Associates and outlined in Infinite Giving's own State of Nonprofit Asset Gifts report.

Let that sink in: $124 trillion. That's trillion with a "T." A massive wave of wealth, not in checking accounts, but in real estate, retirement accounts, stock portfolios, donor-advised funds, and trusts — it's all about to change hands.

Some of that wealth will go to the family, and some to taxes. But a staggering amount will go to charitable organizations, only if those organizations are ready to receive it.

A Gift You Plant, Not Just Pick

Think about legacy giving the same way you might think about planting trees. You don't wait until you're hungry and then plant an apple seed. You prepare the soil. You plant the seed. You water it, nurture it, and eventually, years later, you harvest the fruit.

Legacy gifts, especially from appreciated assets, are no different. You don't wait for donors to bring them up. You start the conversation. You share stories. You make the process easy and compelling. You plant early and often.

What the Data Shows

In his groundbreaking research, Dr. Russell James found that organizations that **actively discussed and promoted planned giving** saw significantly greater long-term fundraising growth than those that didn't.

> "The presence of legacy gifts is one of the strongest predictors of organizational financial growth and resilience."
>
> — Dr. Russell James,
> EncourageGenerosity.com

He also found that the **majority of large charitable estate gifts** came from **donors who had never made a large lifetime donation.** In fact, nearly 90% of estate gifts came from donors whose lifetime giving totaled less than $5,000.

This flips conventional wisdom on its head. It's not just your wealthiest, flashiest supporters who make legacy gifts. It's often your faithful, quiet, long-time givers, the ones who show up, year after year, because they believe in your mission.

But here's the catch: they don't give legacy gifts to organizations that don't talk about them.

Creating a Giving Loop

When nonprofits are prepared to receive asset-based gifts and have a strategy for stewardship, they can create a "Giving Loop" that grows generosity and trust over time.

Here's how the loop works:

- You talk about legacy and non-cash giving openly and early with your donors.

- A donor gives a gift of stock or designates your organization in their will.

- You invest that gift wisely for long-term impact.

- You tell the story of that impact and invite others to join.

- More donors begin to see your organization as a worthy place for legacy giving.

It's a reinforcing cycle of trust, generosity, and impact. And it doesn't just happen with large institutions. **You can build this loop,** even as a small or mid-sized nonprofit.

Don't Wait for the Will

Too many nonprofit boards and leadership teams operate in reactive mode.

They say, *"We'll figure that out if someone wants to leave us something in their will."* Or worse, *"We've never received a stock gift, so we don't need to worry about that right now."*

But that's not how transformational giving works.

Major gifts go to organizations that are ready. Just like we discussed in Chapter 10, not all donors ask, "Can you accept stock?" or "Do you have a brokerage account?" They'll simply assume you don't (or it will be too difficult) and give the gift somewhere else.

With the Great Wealth Transfer underway, this isn't just a missed opportunity. It's a strategic oversight.

3 Practical Ways to Prepare

You don't need a full planned giving department to get started. Here are three foundational ways to prepare your organization to receive legacy and asset-based gifts:

1. Normalize the Conversation

Start talking about legacy giving regularly in your newsletters, your website, donor meetings, and fundraising campaigns. Use warm, inclusive language like:

- "You can make a gift today or leave a legacy for tomorrow."

- "Consider joining our Legacy Circle by making a planned gift."

- "We gratefully accept gifts of stock, DAF grants, and estate gifts."

Make it normal. Make it visible. Then repeat, repeat, repeat.

2. Set Up the Infrastructure

If you don't already have a brokerage account or a relationship with a nonprofit investment advisor, get that in place now. Don't wait for a donor to ask. You'll also want to:

- Draft language for bequest gifts.

- Create a simple one-pager for donors explaining how to make a legacy or asset-based gift.

- Prepare your team and board so they understand the strategy and stewardship needs involved.

3. Celebrate and Steward

If someone does make a legacy or asset gift, even a small one, then celebrate it! Tell the story (with permission). Create a giving society. Use their generosity to inspire others.

Dr. James' research shows that simply **talking about other legacy gifts** significantly increases the likelihood of future legacy giving. Why? Because donors want to be part of a movement. They want to know they're not alone and are in great company.

The Gift of Long-Term Vision

The Great Wealth Transfer is about more than dollars. It's about vision, legacy, and meaningful impact.

You're showing your donors that your mission isn't just about today but the next 50+ years. You're creating something enduring, rooted, and deeply meaningful.

Asset gifts, when stewarded well, can fund scholarships, launch new programs, build endowments, and create financial resilience that your annual budget could never achieve alone.

They are gifts that keep on giving, but you have to be thinking long-term.

Final Thoughts: Build the Bridge Now

If you remember one thing from this chapter, let it be this: **The time to prepare is now.**

The Great Wealth Transfer is not a distant prediction because it's already happening. Every day, donors are making decisions about where their resources will go, how their legacies will be remembered, and which missions they want to sustain long after they're gone. An estimated **$124 trillion** will change hands over the next two decades. The question is, **will your organization be ready to receive it?**

You don't need to be perfect. You don't need a planned giving department or millions already in reserves. What you need is **readiness** and the willingness to say:

Yes to a conversation.
Yes to an unexpected gift.
Yes to the idea that your mission deserves to last.

Because it does. And your donors believe it, too.

With thoughtful planning, strategic stewardship, and a clear, consistent invitation, you can become the kind of organization donors trust with their most meaningful gifts. You can move from passive waiting to proactive readiness.

This is the moment to build the bridge between today's mission and tomorrow's impact.

Don't wait. Signal that you're ready, because generosity flows where it's welcomed.

Key Takeaways for Your Mission

- **The Wealth Transfer Is Already Happening – and Nonprofits Must Be Ready**
  With $124 trillion set to pass between generations in the coming decades, nonprofits have a once-in-a-generation opportunity to receive transformational gifts. Now is the time to prepare with the right infrastructure, messaging, and mindset.

- **Legacy Giving Is for Everyone and Needs to Be Talked About**
  Most major estate gifts don't come from just your wealthy donors but from your modest, consistent donors. Start normalizing the conversation around planned and asset-based giving using clear, inviting language across all donor touchpoints.

- **Readiness Builds Trust and Momentum**
  Nonprofits that actively promote legacy giving and are equipped to accept non-cash gifts create a "Giving Loop" that builds long-term donor trust, deepens relationships, and attracts future gifts.

CHAPTER 12

Built to Last, Built for More

For too long, the nonprofit sector has operated under an invisible weight. A belief that money is something to apologize for. That strength in financial strategy somehow dilutes our moral integrity. That living on the edge of just enough is noble.

But let's be honest, what's noble about instability?

You were not called to burn out. You were not called to run your mission on fumes. And you were not called to say no to opportunity simply because the bank account says so.

This book has walked you through the tools, strategies, and mindset shifts to build something better. Not just for survival but for sustainability, growth, and legacy.

Now, it's time to put it all together. Because money, when stewarded wisely, is one of the most powerful tools your mission can have.

The End of Scarcity Thinking

Scarcity teaches us to do more with less. But strategy teaches us to do more – with purpose.

Many nonprofits have internalized scarcity as a virtue. They celebrate "lean" budgets, spend down every dollar by year-end, and defer investments that could make their teams stronger and their programs more effective. Not because they want to, but because they think they have to.

It's time to break that cycle.

When we normalize financial struggle as part of nonprofit identity, we unintentionally undermine the very missions we're here to protect. Scarcity thinking leads to staff burnout, deferred maintenance, donor mistrust, and missed opportunities. It keeps us stuck in short-term decisions, when what we need is a long-term vision.

Financial strength is not a sign that you're too corporate. It's a sign that your mission matters enough to sustain.

Scarcity → Strategy → Sustainability (Abundance)

This is the journey of leveling up.

We start by shifting from fear to clarity – from apologizing for financial planning to owning it. That's the move from scarcity to strategy. Then, we use that strategy to build structures: reserves, investment policies, Short, Mid, and Long-term strategies, donor-ready systems, and diversified income streams. That's how you move toward sustainability, not abundance for the sake of it, but so your mission never hits a financial ceiling again.

Sustainability is not about hoarding; instead, think of it as preparation. How can you steward today's gifts with tomorrow's impact in mind?

Mission + Money = Real Impact

This isn't about choosing between impact and income because, in reality, they're deeply connected.

- You want to expand your programs? You need margin.

- You want to hire and retain great people? You need stability.

- You want to move fast when opportunity knocks? You need liquidity.

- You want to weather the next crisis? You need a plan.

Nonprofits are doing some of the most important work in the world, and they deserve the same financial sophistication as any business, large foundation, or university.

Let's stop treating excellence in finance as an add-on. It's central to mission effectiveness.

Courageous Leadership Starts Here

The new standard for nonprofit leadership is not only about delivering excellent programs, but it's also about pairing that excellence with bold, strategic financial stewardship. We have to lead courageously with both clarity and compassion.

It takes courage to stand in front of your board and say, "We're building reserves because our mission deserves staying power." It takes courage to shift from passive savings to intentional investment and explain, "We're putting our money to work so our impact can grow."

It takes courage to prepare your systems to receive non-cash gifts and complex assets, not because someone has already offered, but because you believe the offer will come and you want to be ready.

It takes courage to say, out loud, "We believe our mission is worth this kind of strength."

Perhaps most of all, it takes courage to invite generous givers into that vision, not as a plea for help, but as an opportunity to partner in something enduring. When you lead this way, you're not just asking for support, you're casting a vision of legacy and impact that others will want to join.

Let your leadership be defined not by how little you can get by on, but by how wisely and boldly you steward what you've been entrusted with. Because it's not about spending more; instead, think of it as planning to last.

A New Kind of Legacy

At Infinite Giving, we often say that legacy isn't built in one moment; it's built in every decision you make today. Every policy is drafted. Every investment is aligned. And every gift you steward with great care.

You are not just leading a nonprofit. You are shaping a better future for all of us.

One where:

- Financial stability replaces guesswork.

- Mission growth replaces fear.

- Endowments are seeded, not someday, but soon.

- Generous donors give boldly because you're ready to receive boldly.

This is the kind of nonprofit sector we need to build together. One where financial sustainability is built into the foundation of every mission.

Final Thoughts: Funding Your Mission for the Future

Start by believing your organization deserves more than survival. That financial strength and mission strength can, and must, walk hand in hand.

If you've made it to this point in the book, then you've already said yes to a better way forward. You've said yes to building systems that don't just get you through this year but prepare you for the next. You've said yes to leading with financial courage. Now, say yes to putting it into action.

What does it mean to be *built to last and built for more*?

It means your nonprofit is no longer clinging to the edge of every budget cycle. It's standing on solid ground: financially resilient, strategically equipped, and ready to weather any storm.

But it also means you're not stopping there.

You weren't made for maintenance. You were made for momentum.

Being *built for more* means you dream bigger. You invite transformational gifts. You steward your mission with the kind of boldness that inspires others to join you. It's a commitment to sustainability and growth, not as opposites, but as partners.

We know it's not easy, but it is possible, and it is important.

Because nonprofits that last don't just preserve impact. They multiply it.

And that is what you were built for.

From all of us at Infinite Giving, here's to your future: resourced, resilient, and ready for more.

We're here to help you get there.

ACKNOWLEDGEMENTS

First and foremost, to my husband, Paul, and our daughter, Haven, you are my greatest joy. Thank you for the late nights, weekends, and countless small sacrifices that made space for this book and for Infinite Giving. Your love and encouragement remind me of what truly matters. May the work we're building together send ripples of generosity and impact far beyond us.

What I've shared in these pages is not theory, it's lived experience. At Infinite Giving, we walk this out daily. I am deeply grateful to my co-founder Connor Ford, for partnering to build an impactful company; to Lauren Patrick, who made planning and execution of this book possible; to my early readers whose edits made us better, Lynne West, Ross Hendrickson, and Brad Leeper; to our Infinite Giving team working tirelessly every day, we couldn't do this without you. To our Investment Committee, advisors, investors, and every colleague and community member who has locked arms on this mission, you've each played a part in bringing this vision to life.

To our nonprofit clients, you are the heart of this story. Your courage, resilience, and relentless pursuit of impact inspire me more than I can say. It is an honor to serve you.

To our partners, consultants, and advocates, thank you for championing nonprofit sustainability. You have seen what's possible and helped pave the way for others to follow.

A special thank you to Dr. Russell James for your generosity of spirit and wisdom. Your research and example of paying it forward are an invaluable gift to me and the nonprofit community.

I am also grateful to our publishing partners at Stonecrest, Timmy Bauer and Nicole Procopio, for bringing *Funding Your Mission* into the world with excellence and care.

And above all, I'm grateful to God. His faithfulness has carried me every step of the way. This book, like Infinite Giving, is just one small act of stewardship in something far greater than me. The challenges are real, but so is our capacity to meet them. Together, we can build a future where generosity and strategy sustain missions for generations to come.

With gratitude,
Karen

ABOUT THE AUTHOR

Karen Houghton is the CEO and co-founder of Infinite Giving, a Registered Investment Advisor serving mission-driven organizations. A nationally recognized voice on nonprofit finance, Karen has advised hundreds of organizations across the country, equipping leaders with the strategy and tools to build lasting financial health. Previously a nonprofit executive and venture capital leader, Karen bridges the worlds of impact and investment with uncommon clarity. A frequent speaker and trusted advisor, Karen lives in north Atlanta with her husband and daughter.

BIBLIOGRAPHY

- **Association of Fundraising Professionals (AFP) Global.** (2025, February 15). FEP data Q4 2024 highlights the growing role of high-dollar donors driving fundraising performance.

- **Coinbase.** (2025, July). Crypto market update: Bitcoin reaches all-time high.

- **GuideStar, Charity Navigator, & BBB Wise Giving Alliance.** (2013). Letter to the donors of America.

- **Federal Reserve Board.** (2018). Stock ownership is growing: Federal Reserve Survey of Consumer Finances. Investment Company Institute.

- **Infinite Giving.** (2025, June). "State of Nonprofit Asset Giving" report.

- **Merrill Lynch.** (2023). The great wealth transfer: $124 trillion impact.

- **National Council of Nonprofits.** (2023). Nonprofit impact matters: Nonprofits by the numbers.

- **National Philanthropic Trust.** (2023). 2023 donor-advised fund report.

- **Russell N. James III, J.D., Ph.D., CFP** (2018). "Why cash is not king in fundraising: Results from 1 million nonprofit tax returns" [SlideShare presentation].
  o Dr. James – Encourage Generosity – Perceived financial health and donor generosity. https://www.encouragegenerosity.com/

- **The Census Bureau.** (2023). Household wealth in the U.S.: 90% held in non-cash assets.

- **The Giving Block / Galaxy Research.** (2022). Giving in crypto boomed in 2021: $300 million donated.

- **U.S. Trust & Lilly Family School of Philanthropy.** (2021). U.S. Trust study of high net worth philanthropy.

APPENDICES

Meet Your Nonprofit Financial Advisor

Infinite Giving's mission is to transform how nonprofits manage and grow their finances.

As a Registered Investment Advisor created exclusively for nonprofits, we help you easily receive complex gifts, manage your cash reserves, and conservatively invest your funds with one fiduciary partner.

At our core, we believe in the vital work nonprofits do. By fostering strong relationships, increasing transparency and efficiency, and providing thoughtful stewardship, we empower organizations like yours to thrive.

We are the future of nonprofit finance. It would be an honor to serve you.

Scan this QR code to schedule a time and get started with Infinite Giving.

Infinite Giving

www.InfiniteGiving.com

Key Financial Terms Every Nonprofit Leader Should Know

Whether you're sitting in a board meeting discussing risk tolerance or reviewing your nonprofit's liquidity with a financial advisor, the right vocabulary empowers you to ask better questions, make informed decisions, and protect your mission for the long term.

Here are 12 financial terms you should know:

1. **Asset Allocation** – How your investments are divided across different asset classes (like stocks, bonds, and cash). It's key to balancing risk and return based on your goals and time horizons.

2. **AUM (Assets Under Management)** – The total market value of investments a financial advisor or institution manages on behalf of clients. Many advisors charge fees as a percentage of AUM, making it both a measure of portfolio size and a common fee structure in investment management.

3. **Diversification** – Spreading investments across various assets to reduce risk. A diversified portfolio protects your organization from being too dependent on one type of investment.

4. **Endowment** – A permanently or temporarily restricted pool of funds intended to support your mission over the long term, often invested to generate income.

5. **Investment Policy Statement (IPS)** – A governing document that outlines how your nonprofit will manage and invest its assets. It aligns your financial goals with your mission, board oversight, and risk strategy.

6. **Liquidity** – How quickly and easily assets can be converted into cash without losing value. Liquidity matters when determining how accessible your funds are for short-term needs.

7. **Operating Cash Flow (OCF)** – The cash generated or used in day-to-day activities. Understanding your

cash flow helps you plan reserves and avoid overextension.

8. **Rebalancing** – The process of adjusting the mix of assets in a portfolio back to its target allocation to maintain the intended risk and return profile. This should be done regularly and/or at a set threshold.

9. **Reserves** – Set-aside funds that act as a financial cushion for future needs, emergencies, or strategic opportunities. Strong reserves signal organizational health and stability.

10. **Risk Tolerance** – The degree of variability in investment returns your organization can withstand. It's shaped by your mission, board expectations, and financial timeline.

11. **Time Horizon** – The length of time you plan to hold funds before needing them. Matching investments to their time horizon helps guide smart allocation and risk tolerance.

12. **Yield** – The earnings generated from an investment, usually expressed as a percentage. Yield helps nonprofits understand how their money is growing over time.

Financial Framework Checklist

This checklist helps nonprofit leaders evaluate their financial foundation and identify steps to strengthen resilience and long-term impact in key areas:

Diversified Revenue Streams

Ensure your organization is not overly dependent on a single funding source. Consider incorporating multiple income streams, such as:

- Earned income from services, ticket sales, or training programs

- Membership models that provide recurring revenue

- Strategic partnerships with corporations or local businesses

- Government contracts or grants providing stability alongside donations

- Investment income (generated dividends) from reserves, endowments, or other managed funds

New Pathways of Giving

Expand beyond traditional donations to capture generosity in new forms. Evaluate whether your organization can:

- Accept gifts of stock, crypto, or donor-advised fund (DAF) gifts

- Leverage technology platforms to streamline non-cash giving on your website and other marketing platforms

- Promote planned giving options, such as bequests or legacy gifts

- Encourage in-kind donations that reduce operating expenses

- Offer giving opportunities that align with donor values and capacity

Tiered Investment Strategy

- Operating cash flow: Cover immediate expenses and payroll

- Short-term reserves: Maintain at least six months of operating costs in low-risk, liquid accounts

- Mid-term funds: Allocate resources for maintenance, grant matching, or capital campaigns

- Long-term investments: Build endowments or growth-oriented funds to sustain your mission for decades

Diversifying Revenue Worksheet

A financially resilient nonprofit doesn't rely on one source of funding. Use this worksheet to evaluate and expand your revenue streams.

Step 1: Current Snapshot

List your current sources of revenue and estimate the percentage of your total budget they represent.

Revenue Source	% of Budget	Notes
Donations	%	*Individual + major gifts*
Earned income (services, ticket sales, training)	%	*Separate by annual events and source*
Membership models	%	
Strategic partnerships	%	*Include businesses*
Investment income (generated dividends)	%	*reserves, endowment, managed funds*
Government contracts or grants	%	
Other	%	
Total	100%	

Step 2: Current Snapshot

List your current sources of revenue and estimate the percentage of your total budget they represent. For each potential revenue stream below, circle your current status and jot down next steps.

1. **Earned Income (services, ticket sales, training programs)**
   Current Status: Not Started / In Progress / Strong
   Notes: _____

2. **Membership Models (recurring revenue)**
   Current Status: Not Started / In Progress / Strong
   Notes: _____

3. **Strategic Partnerships (corporate, local businesses)**
   Current Status: Not Started / In Progress / Strong
   Notes: _____

4. **Investment Income (reserves, endowments, managed funds)**
   Current Status: Not Started / In Progress / Strong
   Notes: _____

5. **Government Contracts or Grants**
   Current Status: Not Started / In Progress / Strong
   Notes: _____

Step 3: Action Plan

- Which **one or two revenue streams** could you grow in the next 12 months?

- What resources, expertise, or partners do you need to pursue them?

- Who on your team or board will take the lead?

Tip: Revisit this worksheet annually to track progress and ensure your organization is building long-term sustainability.

APPENDIX E

Operating Expense Calculator

The goal of this worksheet is to provide a framework for your nonprofit board or leadership team to review and fill out together. The goal will be to have a true picture of your Operating Expenses, estimate your Cash Runway, and outline the goals for your Cash Reserves.

Step 1: Monthly Averages → Multiply by 12 for Annual Totals

Expense Category	Monthly Average ($)	Annual Expense ($)
Personnel Costs (salaries, benefits, payroll taxes)		
Facilities & Operations (rent/mortgage, utilities, office supplies, insurance)		
Programs & Services (direct program expenses, materials, events)		
Administration (accounting, legal, software, licenses)		
Fundraising & Marketing (campaigns, events, donor stewardship)		

Total Operating Expenses		
Target Reserves (6–12 months of expenses)		

Step 2: Cash Runway Tool (Equation)

To estimate your Cash Runway = you'll divide your Average Monthly Expenses from above with Unrestricted Cash:

- 3 months = survival buffer

- 6 months = recommended minimum

- 12 months = financial strength

Summation:

Unrestricted Cash ÷ Monthly Average = <u>XX</u> months runway

Step 3: Reserve Goal – Create Your Tiered Framework

- **Operating cash flow:** Cover immediate expenses and payroll

- **Short-term reserves:** Maintain at least six months of operating costs in low-risk, liquid accounts

- **Mid-term funds:** Allocate resources for maintenance, grant matching, or capital campaigns

- **Long-term investments:** Build endowments or growth-oriented funds to sustain your mission for decades
  Which tier are you in today? _____
  What's your next target tier? _____

If you need help with your cash management program and reserves, schedule a time to connect with the Infinite Giving team.

Unlocking Donor Advised Fund (DAF) Dollars – Worksheet

This worksheet helps nonprofit leaders improve their DAF giving program by ensuring their organization is visible, accessible, and ready to steward these donors. Use it to track your progress toward capturing more DAFs.

- Register with the "Big Three" sponsors to allow donors to easily find and give to your organization.
  - Fidelity Charitable
  - Schwab Charitable
  - National Philanthropic Trust

- Update your profiles: Keep Guidestar and PayPal Giving Fund information current, as many DAF sponsors pull data directly from these sources.

- Add a DAF giving option online: Include a "Give from your DAF" button or page on your website with links to sponsor portals.
  - If you need help implementing a DAF giving option, please **reach out to us at hello@InfiniteGiving.com**

- Promote stock and crypto to encourage direct giving. Educate donors that they receive the same tax benefit whether they give directly or through a DAF.

- Thank and steward DAF donors personally: They already have charitable funds set aside, making them strong long-term prospects.

Questions for reflection for your development team:

- Which of these steps have we already completed?

- Which areas need immediate attention?

- Who on our team will own each next step to grow our DAF giving?

APPENDIX G

Sample Investment Policy Statement Template

Introduction

The purpose of this Investment Policy Statement is to establish guidelines for [Organization Name]'s Short, Mid, and Long-term financial strategies for reserve funds, growth accounts, and large gifts.

Discuss accountability standards that will be used for monitoring the progress of the organization's cash management and investment program and for evaluating the contributions of the funds and/or advisor(s) hired on behalf of [Organization Name].

1. Role of the Finance Team and Board

Outline who is responsible for financial objectives, distribution policies, and investment guidelines that govern the activities of the Board and any other parties to whom the Board has delegated investment management responsibility for the organization's assets.

    A. It should outline policies and guidelines at a high level

    B. When the Board will review the Policy Statement

    C. How changes will be made and notified

2. Objectives for Cash Reserves

Here, you discuss your strategies for cash management and reserves

    1. Cash holdings

    2. FDIC coverage

    3. Reserve and assets

    4. Funds for the annual operating budget

    5. Board review of budgetary assumptions

    6. Oversight of investment returns

    7. Cash investment strategy

8. Where operational reserves will be maintained, and how many months of funds will be available

3. Objectives for Endowment and Growth Accounts

Discuss holdings and risk tolerance with objectives for long-term growth, providing financial stability and continuity to the organization

1. How fund assets will be placed and managed

2. [Organization Name]'s specifications on strategy for the investment portfolio

3. How withdrawals will be permitted

4. Additional Endowment Policies

5. Information regarding the timing of any distribution(s) from the investment account

4. Asset Allocation Policy

Discuss how the Board recognizes that the strategic allocation of assets across broadly defined financial asset and sub-asset categories with varying degrees of risk, return, and return correlation will be the most significant determinant of long-term returns and Portfolio asset value stability. More goes here about the role of equity investments, where pertinent for your portfolio

5. Asset Allocation Guidelines

Outline strategic asset allocation guidelines determined by the Board to be the most appropriate, given the organization's timelines, risk tolerance, and financial goals across broad asset and sub-asset classes in accordance with the following guidelines:

- **Equities:** range of total assets (%)

- **Fixed Income:** range of total assets (%)

*Specify diversification not to exceed 100%

6. Diversification and Duration Policy

More about the diversification of asset classes and the means by which the Board expects the Portfolio to avoid undue risk of large losses over time.

7. Rebalancing

Outline when the portfolio's actual asset allocation will occur

8. Prohibited Investment Policies

Examples

1. Cash holdings that are not FDIC insured

2. Short-term reserves in holdings that are not fixed income

9. Performance Measurements Standards

For your organization's overall long-term financial objectives, discuss when the Board will evaluate Portfolio and manage performance over a suitably long-term investment horizon. Each investment manager is expected to be available to meet with the leadership and Board once per year (or as needed) to review portfolio structure, strategy, and investment performance.

10. Donor Restrictions

Discuss when donors shall be respected when decisions are rendered concerning the investment or expenditure of donor-restricted funds.

11. Donated Stock and Crypto Policy

Discuss the policy of the organization to liquidate non-cash assets such as stock, crypto, and other marketable securities upon receipt, and then whether you will invest them in cash reserves or further diversified holdings. List where those funds will be transferred.

Infinite Giving provides our clients with complimentary, customized policies unique to their organization.

Ready to get started? Contact us for help creating your nonprofit's IPS.